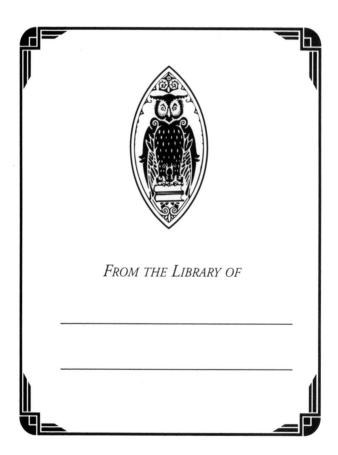

From the Library of

_____

_____

TEACH US TO PRAY

Also by Charles Fillmore

ATOM-SMASHING POWER OF MIND

THE CHARLES FILLMORE CONCORDANCE

CHRISTIAN HEALING

DYNAMICS FOR LIVING

JESUS CHRIST HEALS

KEEP A TRUE LENT

METAPHYSICAL BIBLE DICTIONARY

MYSTERIES OF GENESIS

MYSTERIES OF JOHN

PROSPERITY

THE REVEALING WORD

TALKS ON TRUTH

THE TWELVE POWERS OF MAN

Also by Cora Fillmore

CHRIST ENTHRONED IN MAN

TEACH US TO PRAY

CHARLES AND CORA
FILLMORE

Unity Classic Library

UNITY® Books

Unity Village, Missouri

Teach Us to Pray is a member of the Unity Classic Library.

The Unity Classic Library is guided by the belief of Unity cofounder Charles Fillmore that "whatever God has revealed to man in one age He will continue to reveal to him in all ages." The series projects Fillmore's vision of Unity as "a link in the great educational movement inaugurated by Jesus Christ" to help and teach humankind to use and prove eternal Truth.

To receive a catalog of all Unity publications (books, cassettes, compact discs, and magazines) or to place an order, call the Customer Service Department: 816-969-2069 or 1-800-669-0282. For information, address Unity Books, Publishers, Unity School of Christianity, 1901 NW Blue Parkway, Unity Village, MO 64065-0001.

First printing 1941; twenty-first printing 2002

Marbled design by Mimi Schleicher © 1994
Cover design by Jill L. Ziegler

Library of Congress Control Number: 2001098729
ISBN: 0-87159-203-7
Canada BN 13252 9033 RT

Unity Books feels a sacred trust to be a healing presence in the world. By printing with biodegradable soybean ink on recycled paper, we believe we are doing our part to be wise stewards of our Earth's resources.

"We must know first that prayer is cumulative; that the more we pray, the more we accumulate of the powerful spiritual energy which transforms invisible ideas into visible things."

Charles Fillmore

Cora Fillmore

FOREWORD

→»«←

When Jesus' disciples asked Him to teach them how to pray He warned them against making a display of their praying in order to be seen of men. They should retire to their "inner chamber" and pray to the Father who sees in secret and rewards openly. Then He said, "After this manner therefore pray." The Lord's Prayer was given as a sample: not to be followed literally. It is a petition according to the American revision; but according to Fenton's translation it is a series of affirmations, as follows:

"Our Father in the Heavens; Your Name must be being hallowed;

"Your kingdom must be being restored;

"Your will must be being done, both in Heaven and upon the Earth.

"Give us to-day our to-morrow's bread;

"And forgive us our faults, as we forgive those offending us, for You would not lead us into temptation, but deliver us from its evil."

As in all matters where we seek divine help we are free to use any words we choose or no words at all.

"Prayer is the soul's sincere desire,
Uttered or unexpressed."

Prayer in man is a conscious expression of the upward trend of nature found everywhere. So every impulse or desire of the soul for life, love, light, is a prayer.

Eliphaz repeated a prayer formula when he said, "Thou shalt also decree a thing, and it shall be established unto thee."

Jesus put the same idea in these words: "Whatsoever ye shall ask in my name, that will I do."

All growth and unfoldment from atom to sun is based upon this law of soul urge.

What you earnestly desire and persistently affirm will be yours, if you "faint not."

When we frame our desires in sound words and place them before our indwelling Lord, we are using intelligently the supreme law of God in bringing into manifestation that which He has implanted in us.

A prayer without desire in it, a prayer without sincerity in it, a prayer without soul in it, a prayer without Spirit in it is a fruitless prayer.

But above all practice the presence of God in prayer. Divine Mind has given us all potentialities, in prayer we recognize it as the source of these, and with a right understanding of our relation to it our soul grows great with infinite capacity, all potentiality. "With God all things are possible." "All things whatsoever the Father hath are mine."

We have been so persistently taught that prayer consists in asking God for some human need that we have lost sight of our spiritual identity and have become a race of praying beggars. God is Spirit in whom we "live, and move, and have our being." We are the offspring of this Spirit and can make conscious contact with it by turning our attention away from material things and thinking about Spirit. As we practice this kind of prayer our innate Spirit showers its life energies into our conscious mind and a great soul expansion follows.

Jesus described this in the following words:

"But thou, when thou prayest, enter into thine inner chamber, and having shut thy door, pray to thy Father who is in secret, and thy Father who seeth in secret shall recompense thee."

This "inner chamber" of the soul has been variously named by Scripture writers. It is called the "secret place of the Most High" and the "holy of holies," and Jesus named it "the Father . . . in me" and "the kingdom of God . . . within you." What we need to know above all is that there is a place within our soul where we can consciously meet God and receive a flood of new life into not only our mind but also our body.

This understanding shows us that prayer is more than asking God for help in this physical world; it is in its highest sense the opening up in our soul of an innate spiritual umbilical cord that connects us with the Holy Mother, from whom we can receive a perpetual flow of life. This is the beginning of eternal life for both soul and body, the essential teaching of Jesus, which He demonstrated in overcoming death.

We have earnestly sought to know and tell others how to pray, and this book is our very best exposition of the subject. Language has not yet been invented to tell all the wonders that we have found since we began opening our minds to the Spirit in prayer. We have discovered enough to convince us that the body can be so charged with spiritual life through prayer that it will overcome death, as promised by Jesus Christ.

Do not enlarge the defects of this book until they darken its truths, but accept the urge to begin the practice of prayer and through it make contact with the source of your being. Thus you will prove that, as Job wisely taught,

"There is a spirit in man,

And the breath of the Almighty giveth them understanding."

CONTENTS

The God to Whom We Pray

>>><<<

Earth's crammed with heaven,
And every common bush afire with God;
But only he who sees takes off his shoes,
The rest sit round it and pluck blackberries.
—Elizabeth Browning

OMNIPRESENCE, omniscience, omnipotence are verities of Being and are facts of existence. The Mind of God, creative Mind, is perpetually moving upon supermind ideas and through them bringing man and the universe into existence.

Creative Mind is everywhere present; yet while it is within the mind of man it lies beyond the consciousness of sense.

Omnipresence is that spiritual realm which can be penetrated only through the most highly accelerated mind action, as in prayer. Thus in unfolding this inner kingdom we are dealing with a reality beyond the ordinary comprehension of man.

To the superbly tuned mind and brain of Jesus Divine Mind was a soil eager with vibrant life and light and substance, which He used to produce the finest of materials for both character and body building.

Spiritual character building is from within out-

ward. Spiritual character lives in man; it is what
God has engraved on man's soul, ready for development through man's spiritual efforts. It is a reserve
force of organized victory over carnality.

Man builds spiritual character by consciously
functioning in God-Mind, where, laying hold of spiritual ideas, through Christ he realizes the Truth they
contain; and as he thus weaves them into his soul
consciousness they become a part of his very nature.

Our most effective prayers are those in which we
rise above all consciousness of time and space. In
this state of mind we automatically contact the Spirit
of God. Indeed when we elevate our consciousness
to that of Jesus Christ, the God presence becomes
as meaningful to us as it was to Him. It is in this
state of at-one-ment that we truly become aware of
His sublimity and power.

"I go to prepare a place for you." By getting ac-
quainted with the one Mind as integral substance,
we move with it and it moves with us, and thus are
established within us new spiritual states of consciousness, a "place" where we are aware of the
God presence as reality.

Jesus said: "My Father is the husbandman." "I
am the true vine." "Ye are the branches." "As the
branch cannot bear fruit of itself, except it abide in
the vine; so neither can ye, except ye abide in me."

"Every branch in me that beareth not fruit, he
taketh away: and every *branch* that beareth fruit,
he cleanseth it, that it may bear more fruit."

In this scripture Jesus is revealing to us that

through Him we are born anew, born of God, and
that through Him we may be consciously attached
to God—as the branch is attached to the tree—so
that we may not wither and be cast away.

Through Christ we are consciously attached to
the parent stem. It behooves us to retain this attach-
ment so that we may go forward in spiritual unfoldment and be crowned with eternal life.

Many good people think that God is a person
located in a place in the skies called heaven. They
pray to Him for what they want and are satisfied.
This is the prayer of the primitive, personal man,
and it meets his needs; but this is not direct communion of the Father and the Son, the communion
with reference to which Jesus said, "I and the Father
are one." We must have this more intimate ac-
quaintanceship or communion with creative Mind if
we are in all ways to do His will.

God presence establishes us in ideas of honesty,
strength, intelligence, spiritual manhood, perfect
womanhood, all needed factors in the unfoldment
of the redeemed man, all builders of the indestruct-
ible body temple.

Thus we must understand the nature of the God
to whom we pray and awaken in ourselves that divine
nature through which we effect our union with God.

God is power: man is powerful. God is wisdom:
man is wise. God is substance: man is form and
shape. God is love: man is loving. God is life: man
is the living. God is mind: man is the thinker. God
is truth: man is truthful.

Many people pray to God in the same manner as they talk to some distant friend over the telephone. We talk too much about God, too much as though He were a third person in the God-man relationship instead of the first. It is unthinkable that the Creator should cause to exist a creation so inferior to Himself as to remove it beyond the pale of fellowship with Him. In his saner moments man knows that this is not logical or true. It is man's exalted ideas of God and his disparaging ideas of himself that have built the mental wall that separates them.

In our prayers we must meet God face to face and realize that we are getting that inner assurance which is the real answer to our petitions.

A minister, after twenty years of faith preaching, once was persuaded by a friend to try the Truth way of prayer, the way of scientific silence. Afterwards he confessed that when he touched God and found Him alive he was startled.

To Jesus the God presence was an abiding flame, a flame of life, of life everlasting that He felt in every cell and fiber of His being, making Him more and more alive, cleansing and purifying until He became every whit perfect. During our higher realizations of Truth we are often conscious of this abiding flame working in us and through us.

To Jesus God-Mind was a treasure field within Him in which could be found the fulfillment of every need He could possibly have. The Spirit of God in Him was constantly working, yes, steadily and persistently working, to transmute every natural impulse of mind and soul into a spiritual realization of life. To Him the Spirit of God was working to satisfy His inner craving with living substance and intelligence, thus rounding out soul and body consciousness into the perfect expression of Divine Mind itself. What a glorious satisfaction God must feel in His perfect Son Jesus who acknowledged His inner consciousness as one with, and as consciously expressing, God's will and wisdom. God Spirit, God-Mind, is not in any way confined or limited; it is everywhere present. The "ether" of science corresponds to "the kingdom of the heavens" taught by Jesus. Light and other forms of radiant energy, the objective expression of the invisible spiritual forces, compose an omnipresent world more marvelous than the old-time heaven. All the forces of modern scientific discovery are but parts of "the kingdom of the heavens" described in the many parables of Jesus. Science recognizes the physical phases of the kingdom, ignores the mental, and utterly fails to comprehend the spiritual.

The announcement of Jesus to the obtuse Nicodemus, "Ye must be born anew," gives us a clue to the shortsightedness of physicists. They have not developed the faculties of mind necessary to the discernment of the spiritual intelligence that moves the physical universe, consequently they see its material aspects only. A new school of science must be developed in which the mind of the Spirit will be given first place.

True Prayer

Truth is within ourselves; it takes no rise
From outward things, whate'er you may believe.
There is an inmost center in us all,
Where truth abides in fulness;
. . . and, to know,
Rather consists in opening out a way
Whence the imprisoned splendor may escape,
Than in effecting entry for a light
Supposed to be without.
— Robert Browning

ALL DOWN the ages man has been making the spiritual effort to realize conscious union with that innermost center where Truth in all its glory abides eternally. This realization can be accomplished only through true prayer.

The disciples of Jesus earnestly importuned, "Lord, teach us to pray." Today, as disciples of the Master, we are asking of Him to be taught the way of unifying our consciousness with God-Mind. We would find that inner Truth which sets us free.

His instructions to the disciples were "But thou, when thou prayest, enter into thine inner chamber, and having shut thy door, pray to thy Father who is in secret, and thy Father who seeth in secret shall recompense thee." It is difficult to improve upon

16

this simple method. Quietly entering the inner chamber within the soul, shutting the door to the external thoughts of daily life, and seeking conscious union with God is the highest form of prayer we know.

The purpose of the silence is to still the activity of the individual thought so that the still small voice of God may be heard. For in the silence Spirit speaks Truth to us and just that Truth of which we stand in need.

Prayer is man's steady effort to know God. There is an intimate connecting spirit that logically unites man and his source. This connecting spirit is the divine Logos, the Word of God, which in truth reveals the logic of Scripture. Because of this fact man instinctively feels and knows whence his help comes.

God-Mind, composed of radiant ideas, vibrant life, glorious new inspiration, is ours to use. Since we are the *I will* man in the supreme Godhead, let us through Jesus Christ realize our spiritual importance. Let us think deeply on the divine Logos, the Word of God! In it is the living impetus that is bound to vitalize the soul of man and enable him to develop his latent powers.

When we awaken even a very slight consciousness of this co-operative spirit, we become cocreators with God, and we find we can adjust any condition that comes into our life. Jesus was so completely unified with God-Mind that He could claim the words He spoke to be not His but those of the Father dwelling within Him.

Through prayer we gain the intimate relationship with God that Jesus must have enjoyed when He said, "I and the Father are one." Jesus Christ is our teacher and helper. In prayer what should be our attitude, our interest, as we approach the divine presence? If we knew that right now we were about to be ushered into the presence of Christ, to what extent would our spiritual expectancy be aroused? No doubt we should be thrilled through and through at the mere thought. Let us feel this same intense interest, this same concern, as we approach the divine presence within ourselves. It will add much to the readiness with which we receive Truth.

ENTERING THE SILENCE

When entering the silence, according to Hosea, the command is "Take with you words, and return unto Jehovah." After many centuries this instruction still stands approved today. To the metaphysician it means to close the eyes and ears to the without, to go within and hold the mind steadily on the word "Jehovah" until that word illumines the whole inner consciousness. Then affirm a prayer such as *"Thy vitalizing energy floods my whole consciousness, and I am healed."*

Think what the mighty vitalizing energy of God, released through Jesus Christ, really is. Penetrate deeper into God consciousness within you and hold the prayer steadily until you attain spiritual realization and the logic of your own mind is satisfied.

To realize an idea in the silence is to clothe it with life, substance, and intelligence. To realize a prayer is to actualize it. To realize it is to clothe it with soul, to know there is fulfillment.

The word of prayer has in it a living seed that is bound to impregnate the soil of the mind and cause it to bring forth fruit after its kind.

Through Christ man has the power to realize that as I AM or I AM "vitalizing health" he is the great central magnet functioning in omnipresence, around which all the healing powers of Spirit revolve. He has the power to realize this truth until the most sacred ethers respond, and he beholds himself as powerful, peaceful, perfect: healed through and through. It is after this fashion that we engraft the healing word into our very souls.

When we were in Florida a few years ago a citrus fruit grower told us many interesting things about the growth of his orchards. There are many swamps in Florida. He had instructed his men to go out into these swamps, into the muddy black waters infested with creeping things, there to dig up the wild-lemon saplings with their strong, vigorous roots, to transplant them into well-prepared soil, and then to graft into them buds from his prize domestic fruit trees. Thus new trees laden with golden fruit appeared in due time. The strong, vigorous root of the wild lemon gave the new fruit added flavor and quality.

Metaphysically the law is "If the root is holy, so are the branches." At least the branches are potentially holy. We find that the natural man is usually physically strong and vigorous just as the root of the wild-lemon tree is. The natural man also struggles in a murky, negative, swampy atmosphere without power to bring forth spiritually, just as the wild-lemon sapling does.

But the natural man can take a word of Truth and through "one-pointed" mind concentration can penetrate into the invisible, can unite his consciousness with the mind of God, and can hold a realizing prayer until the truth it contains is engrafted into his very soul. Thus just as the citrus fruit is developed through the grafting process, so man, through the engrafted word, becomes a strong, positive spiritual character.

There is only one God, only one ruling power in all the universe; and the highest avenue through which God can express Himself is man. The hungering for God that is felt by man in his soul is really God hungering to express eternal life through man. God is always seeking to awaken man's very soul to His mighty presence. He thus expands the consciousness, offering man an opportunity more fully and more perfectly to express Him.

There is a partial unity with Spirit and there is a complete unity with Spirit. Whenever we wholly merge our mind with creative Mind we meet Christ in our consciousness, and it is when we are in this consciousness that our prayers are fulfilled. The ability to merge our mind into the one Mind makes a great man of us.

Every person hungers for eternal life, and in his effort to satisfy this hunger every soul makes its own concept of God. The ancients said that an honest man is the noblest work of God. Ingersoll said, "An honest God is the noblest work of man."

In deed and in truth prayer is man's spiritual approach to God, and effective prayer does not agonize. Neither Jesus nor any man who has fused his soul with the soul of God has suffered or agonized. The suffering comes as a result of separation and the effort to return to the consciousness of Omnipresence, "my Father's house."

Carlyle said, "Consider the significance of *silence:* it is boundless, never by meditating to be exhausted, unspeakably profitable to thee! Cease that chaotic hubbub, wherein thy own soul runs to waste, to confused suicidal dislocation and stupor; out of silence comes thy strength. Speech is silvern, silence is golden; speech is human, silence is divine.

"Fool! thinkest thou that because no one stands near with parchment and black lead to note thy jargon, it therefore dies and is harmless? Nothing dies, nothing can die. No idlest word thou speakest but is a seed cast into Time, and grows through all eternity. The recording angel, consider it well, is no fable, but the truest of truths; the paper tablets thou canst burn; of the 'iron leaf' there is no burning."

Intellectual Silence and Spiritual Silence

→≫≪←

I T IS MAN'S concept of God that makes prayer intellectual or spiritual. There is a vast difference between mere intellectual silence and that constructive silence which always gives the victory within the soul. The intellectual silence, which is limited in its power, is the silence where one's whole attention is fixed on the intellect.

Herbert Spencer once said that he would gladly turn his life over to anyone who would live it for him and relieve him of its burdens. This no doubt can be said of hundreds of other weary ones. It reveals however the fact that man lacks the true vision of life and is not living it as God intended. Man should lift his eyes "unto the hills, from whence cometh" his help. He should dwell much on the truths taught by Jesus and make them a part of his very nature.

Jesus ushered into the race consciousness a thought atmosphere that we contact in the silence by just affirming in spirit and in truth the name "Jesus Christ." There is true magic in this name.

When He said, "Come unto me, all ye that labor and are heavy laden, and I will give you rest," He was mentally freeing man from his many trials and tribulations, and leading him into the broad highway of spiritual freedom, and joy, and abundance. To accept Jesus Christ as Saviour means to take His way of thinking and acting and make it ours.

There is a popular teaching that just accepting Jesus Christ as one's Saviour will set into operation a spiritual magic that will save the soul from all past and future sins. The word "magic" implies accomplishing something with the assistance of the supernatural. We find that in deed and in truth there is magic in adopting the way of life taught by Jesus. But this is not mysterious to those who study the transforming power of thoughts and words. It is all contained in the formula stated by Paul "Be ye transformed by the renewing of your mind." Instead of doubting, distrusting, and hating man, which is the fruit of the intellect, Jesus taught us to love man with all our mind, soul, and strength. Instead of fighting life and struggling to compete with millions of others in the same foolish war, as the intellectual man does, Jesus taught man to co-operate. Instead of wasting energy in tearing down, Jesus taught man to conserve his energy in building up. Jesus does not load on man's back all the burdens of humanity; in fact He shows humanity how to love life, how to love the Author of life, and how to love life's activities. In this state of consciousness man automatically drops the burdens of the intellect and enters into the freedom of real living. In the past the intellect has thought its power supreme. But while it is a wonderful faculty, it is in truth the tool of Spirit, and as such it needs discipline if it is to be able to perform its perfect work.

The intellect is always busy, jumping from one thing to another, much of the time dwelling on the daily routine of the workaday world or on conditions in the world at large. The first step in scientific silence is simply to still these outer intellectual thoughts so that the consciousness may become subservient to the Spirit within.

In I Peter 2:2 we read, "As newborn babes, long for the spiritual milk which is without guile, that ye may grow thereby unto salvation." Those who are seeking and receiving spiritual understanding are born anew every day, and every day the milk of the spiritual word continues to feed and nourish the soul.

Moses was commanded by Jehovah to make all things after the pattern shown him on the mount. In the heavens of the mind, the spiritual center in the crown of the head, the Lord keeps ever before man life's perfect pattern. But man must have the spiritual ability to discern this pattern if he is to fulfill the requirements of scientific prayer.

By quieting the mental man, by passing through the discipline of intellectual silence, man arrives at the very threshold of God's workshop, the threshold of Being. As he passes into the inner chamber he finds he is entering the holy of holies, where noiselessly, silently a mighty work is always going on but where there is "neither hammer nor axe nor any tool of iron heard." God works in the stillness. As man comes into the presence of God with his

prayer in the form of an affirmation of Truth, holding the prayer steadily in mind and consciously
unifying his mind with the mind of God, he is aware
only of the soundlessness of God's word as it weaves
itself in and out through the whole soul and body
consciousness, illumining, redeeming, and restoring
him according to his faith and trust, according to his
strength and power to receive. This is quite different
from mere intellectual silence that does not know
the way of spiritual unfoldment. In this spiritual
silence man's realization is established in his heart
and he has the assurance that his prayer is answered
and that the law of demonstration brings forth the
fruit.

The realization is not only written in the soul but
in the intellect, whose seat of action is in the front
forehead. The intellect always perceives what has
taken place within and has power to retain its per-
ception and to express itself accordingly. Thus the
intellect serves Spirit, and as it unfolds it becomes
more and more like Spirit, and it becomes in deed
and in truth the instrument of God.

Carlyle must have had an intellectual understanding as well as a spiritual understanding of divine
law when he wrote, referring to the kingdom within:
"Art not thou the living government of God? O
Heaven, is it not in very deed He then that ever
speaks through thee—that lives and loves in thee—
that lives and loves in me?"

Constructive thought force is a great and mighty
power, but when it is realized in the silence it be-

comes the one and only power in all the earth. The understanding of this made Jesus an adept in the domain of scientific prayer.

"The God that made the world and all things therein, he, being Lord of heaven and earth, dwelleth not in temples made with hands." Jesus was born down among the animals in the manger at Bethlehem. There is a truth symbolized in this; for not only the intellect in man is to be redeemed through prayer but also the body; even every animal propensity must be redeemed and lifted up through Jesus Christ. "In the name of Jesus every knee should bow . . . and . . . every tongue should confess that Jesus Christ is Lord, to the glory of God the Father."

Healing through the Prayer of Faith

→»«←

Is any among you suffering? let him pray. Is any cheerful? let him sing praise. Is any among you sick? let him call for the elders of the church: and let them pray over him, anointing him with oil in the name of the Lord: and the prayer of faith shall save him that is sick, and the Lord shall raise him up.—James

THIS IS A very definite and wonderful promise. According to the record, it was undoubtedly acted upon by the disciples and proved to be very effective for hundreds of years. That this mighty promise still stands is proved by unnumbered thousands of Jesus' followers today. Faith healing through prayer has become a practice founded on principles that never fail when rightly applied. Those who seek the kingdom of God and His righteousness are having all things added, as promised. When we "take with us words" and attempt to go into God's presence, our faith in Him is the power that swings wide open the gate that leads into the inner kingdom.

But in order to keep the gate ajar it is a daily necessity to withdraw into this deep stillness of the soul. Listen first to the innate voice of faith; then through the centers within the subconsciousness you can appropriate the life, substance, and intelligence of Being.

Man builds up an enduring state of faith by repeated realizations of Truth. The illumination thus gained comes forth in man as spiritual understanding expressed in sound words.

Faith draws upon substance. Dynamic, creative, transforming power is roused to spiritual action when man affirms his unity with Almightiness and his undaunted faith in its power.

"Seek good, and not evil, that ye may live; and so Jehovah, the God of hosts, will be with you, as ye say." "Concerning the works of my hands, command ye me."

Man must not only be submissive and obedient to the divine law; he must also realize that he is the offspring of the ruler of the universe.

When asking the Father for that which belongs to the Son under the divine law, man should assume the power and dignity of the Prince of Peace. He should not crawl and cringe before an imaginary king on a throne but rather feel that he is the image of an invisible being who has created him to represent His mightiness as well as His loving-kindness. We should affirm with conviction those mighty words uttered by Jesus: "All authority hath been given unto me in heaven and on earth."

The prayer of faith is not supplication, a begging God to give things to man. Prayer at its highest is the entry of the ego through faith into a realm of mind forces that when rightly contacted change the character of every cell in brain and body. One who has mastered even the primary technique of prayer has made contact with the spiritual ethers that connect all minds, high and low, and by means of which great reforms for the good of man can be projected into the world's thought ether.

When Jesus prayed, sometimes the whole night long, He did not plead with God over and over to do what He asked. Through positive faith Jesus was laying hold of new ideas, which through His spiritual understanding He incorporated into His consciousness, which included both soul and body. Through this mental process He became a living demonstration of spiritual man.

Today Jesus Christ is our helper and teacher. Every man when he prays should recognize and take advantage of this truth. He can profit much by realizing that the same Spirit is in him that was in Jesus, who became the Christ. Paul wrote, "But if the Spirit of him that raised up Jesus from the dead dwelleth in you, he that raised up Christ Jesus from the dead shall give life also to your mortal bodies through his Spirit that dwelleth in you."

Jesus is teaching us today that to pray effectively we must believe and know that there is a dispenser of the thing asked for and that by reaching out in prayer we can receive it from the one great source. This is truly the prayer of faith. "All things whatsoever ye pray and ask for, believe that ye receive them, and ye shall have them."

Faith, the conviction of a higher providing source, is based upon spiritual logic or innate reason and on the certainty that an all-wise and all-powerful Creator's plan includes necessary provision for His offspring. Among even the primitive forms of nature this providing law is active. The insect stores food in the egg for the sustenance of its progeny. When man emerges from his animal consciousness and feels within him the stirring of Spirit, he finds that it is supremely logical and true that Spirit has provided for his supply and support.

When we have achieved spiritual realization of our prayer and our innermost soul is satisfied, we have the assurance that the thing is accomplished in Spirit and must become manifest.

We may continue in our realization of faith until the whole consciousness responds and the instantaneous demonstration takes place.

Spiritual Truth, psychology, and science tell us that visible things come from the invisible and are dependent upon the unseen for their existence. The sense mind cannot conceive of this.

"But there is a spirit in man,
   And the breath of the Almighty giveth them understanding."

Before man can fully appreciate and work the spiritual law, he must cultivate a consciousness of reality. When he does this, he finds he is automatically working with God, through Christ, and that he can say with Jesus, "My Father worketh even until now, and I work."

Prayer is impotent and unfruitful when the one who prays is without the firm belief that his petitions are answered. When man turns wholeheartedly to God, the prayer of faith brings forth abundantly. Healing currents of life are freed and flow into and through soul and body, healing, redeeming, uplifting the whole man. Since the prayer of faith is the activity of divine love, let us pray without ceasing, knowing that God hears and grants our petitions.

Truly the Lord is in the midst of us. When we turn toward the omnipresent light of Spirit in faith, our eyes are opened to the astonishing fact that this seemingly material body and these temporal surroundings conceal the immanent God. We come to understand what Jacob meant when he said, "How dreadful is this place! this is none other than the house of God, and this is the gate of heaven."

In prayer attention is the concentration of the mind upon a statement of Truth. Attention is focalizing the I AM or inner entity upon a word of prayer, until the inner meaning is realized and the soul is aware of a definite spiritual uplift. As a lens focalizes the sun's rays at a given point—and we know how intense that point of light may become —so concentration focalizes the mind on a single idea until it becomes manifest and objective.

In concentration the Holy Spirit works through the divine mother substance to bring forth the fruits of Divine Mind. The Holy Spirit is the teacher. The teacher and the student use the same principles;

but the teacher arouses and inspires the student to greater achievement. The Holy Spirit today is urging us to greater spiritual effort.

When we direct the mental powers upon a definite idea, faith plays its part; it is involved in concentration. As we give attention to the idea through one-pointed mind concentration, we break into a realm of finer mind activity, called faith or the fire of Spirit. Thus faith opens the door into an inner consciousness, where we hold the word steadily in mind until the spiritual ethers respond to our word. Earnest, steady, and continued attention along this line is bound to bring forth the fruits of the Spirit in abundant measure. A steady, unwavering devotion of heart and principle to Spirit develops in us supermind qualities.

Prosperity through Prayer

→→>‹‹‹←

"NOW THERE cried a certain woman of the wives of the sons of the prophets unto Elisha, saying, Thy servant my husband is dead; and thou knowest that thy servant did fear Jehovah: and the creditor is come to take unto him my two children to be bondmen. And Elisha said unto her, What shall I do for thee? tell me; what hast thou in the house? And she said, Thy handmaid hath not anything in the house, save a pot of oil. Then he said, Go, borrow thee vessels abroad of all thy neighbors, even empty vessels; borrow not a few. And thou shalt go in, and shut the door upon thee and upon thy sons, and pour out into all those vessels; and thou shalt set aside that which is full. So she went from him, and shut the door upon her and upon her sons; they brought the *vessels* to her, and she poured out. And it came to pass, when the vessels were full, that she said unto her son, Bring me yet a vessel. And he said unto her, There is not a vessel more. And the oil stayed. Then she came and told the man of God. And he said, Go, sell the oil, and pay thy debt, and live thou and thy sons of the rest."

The story of Elisha and the little pot of oil that at his command and with her co-operation filled all the vessels in her house and also those of all her neighbors so that she had enough oil to pay all her debts, free her children from bondage, and provide a living for herself and her sons, reveals the working of a mighty law.

Metaphysically the meaning of the name Elisha is "God is a savior; God of deliverance; to whom God gives victory; God is rich." The widow typifies a belief in lack, a thought or a line of thought in consciousness that has fallen away from that inner union with the divine source (husband) and as a result is suffering from lack of supply.

Elisha (meaning also "God is rich") showed this woman how to shut the door and realize that her supply came from within. Then he revealed to her how to pour out the oil (love) of plenty, and how it would prove a permanent supply. Any thought is a prayer in which we realize that our desires, God directed, are answered the very moment they are expressed.

Christian metaphysicians find that words that express thanks, gratitude, and praise, release energies of mind and spirit, and their use is usually followed by effects so pronounced that they are quickly identified with the originating words, effect being merged in cause.

Let your words of praise and blessing be to Spirit and the increase will be even greater than it is when they are addressed to man. The resources of Spirit are beyond our highest flights of imagination. You can praise a weak body into strength; a fearful heart into peace and trust; shattered nerves into poise and power; a failing business into prosperity and success; want and insufficiency into supply and support.

Do not beg in your prayers, but praise and give thanks for the new self-manifesting God of abundance fulfilling every desire of your heart.

Make a "date" daily with God and keep it. He will never fail you. Some persons are overtimid about their religion. They fear ridicule and misunderstanding. A certain banker had established a certain time each day for going into the silence to pray. His bank, which was located in a country town, needed to borrow what it considered a large sum of money, and he was in New York City negotiating for the loan, but without apparent success. However he was strong in the silence and trusted God regardless of appearances. While he was talking the matter of the loan over with the New York City banker his "silence hour" approached, and our country banker was puzzled what to do. He finally decided to be honest with God, and in the midst of the apparently unfavorable discussion in regard to the loan, he quietly announced that he always devoted a few moments to prayer at that hour and begged to be excused.

The face of the city banker at once lighted up. He instantly recognized that this country friend had something that he did not have: he was poised, peaceful, trustful in the face of defeat. So the city banker hesitatingly replied that he also was in the

habit of observing a daily moment of prayer and
that he would gladly join him. Then and there they
entered the silence together and had a high realization of God's power to supply and to bless. At the
conclusion of their prayer session the city banker
informed the country banker that he was satisfied
that his securities were good and that the loan would
be made without delay.

Emerson's inspiration or comment on prayer was
"Prayer is the contemplation of the facts of life
from the highest point of view. Prayer is the soliloquy of a beholding and jubilant soul. It is the Spirit
of God pronouncing His works good. But prayer as
a means of effecting a private end is theft and
meanness. It presupposes dualism and not unity in
nature and consciousness. As soon as a man is at
one with God he does not beg. He then sees prayer
in all action."

> *Father Almighty! We bow before Thine in-
> finite goodness, and invoke in prayer Thine all-
> merciful presence of love.*
>
> *We ask, and as we ask we give thanks that
> Thy power and presence are here in love and
> that we are tightly held in Thine all-embracing
> arms, where our every need is supplied and
> where we shall ever rest secure from all the
> buffets of the world.*
>
> *Open to us the inner chambers of peace and
> harmony, which divinely belong to us as Thy
> children.*

We come as little children into the sacred and trustful presence of Thy love, knowing full well that only love can draw and hold us in peace and harmony and prosperity.

Every fear falls away as we enter into Thee and Thy glory of love and as we bask in the sunshine of love, Thy love, Thy never-failing love!

Contacting Spiritual Substance

→≫≪←

M AN MUST build a perfect soul structure with faculties capable of always producing abundantly for both his spiritual and his material welfare.

In order to accomplish this man must become familiar with what the metaphysician terms omnipresent Spirit substance, which is visible only to mind and the nature of which is to sustain and enrich whatever idea is projected into it.

This Spirit substance stands back of and gives support to man's every thought and word. It is ready to provide food for all living creatures everywhere.

Today man is learning consciously to make union with this invisible spiritual thought stuff and appropriate and manifest it. Our supply and support is governed by our familiarity with substance and by our mental hold upon it.

Spiritual substance is the source of all material wealth and cannot suffer loss or destruction by human thought. It is always with us, ready to be used and to make potent and fertile both the soul and the body consciousness. In this connection Jesus said, "I have meat to eat that ye know not."

Just as God has been from the beginning so Spirit substance has been from the beginning. This substance is in fact the Mother side of God, the feminine element in God's nature. It is the universal medium in which we plant all ideas of supply and support.

Just as the earth is the universal matrix in which all vegetation develops so this invisible Spirit substance is the universal matrix in which ideas of prosperity germinate and grow and bring forth according to our faith and trust. The "dust of the ground" spoken of in Genesis represents the radiant substance, the fruit of the initial thought in the expression of the substance idea. Under the influence of man's mind radiant Spirit substance continues to be manifested in form and shape. For example, the sunshine is incorporated in the products of the vegetable world; these being appropriated by man through mastication, digestion, and assimilation, it becomes part of his body. Light and electricity are forms of radiant substance.

Someone has said,

> "The hand that rocks the cradle
> Is the hand that rules the world."

In this same way the Mother side of God may be said to cradle our good, nurturing it into manifestation and producing the influences that hover over and enrich our life. We should always bear in mind that if we are to demonstrate we must pay strict attention to the conservation of the spiritual thought stuff. If we are to go forward spiritually, we must not waste our thought stuff in idle thoughts, in thinking thoughts of poverty, discontent, jealousy. We should positively weed out of consciousness all thoughts of poverty and failure, and in thinking or speaking of our affairs we should use the very highest and best language at our command.

Whatever the seed word is that is implanted in omnipresent Spirit substance, this seed word will germinate and grow and bring forth fruit "after its kind." Just as the farmer therefore selects the very best seed corn for planting, so we must choose the words that will bring forth the rich harvest of plenty.

We should bear in mind that God is our silent partner and that His wisdom and strength, His energy and skill are ours to use. We should realize that in every soul there is undoubtedly present (as a result of former effort) a great reservoir of radiant Spirit substance, which is ready and eager to be tapped and freed so that it can supply our every need.

To gain control of Spirit substance we grasp it with our mind; that is, lay hold of the idea back of it. Right thinking is necessary in using the mind constructively to bring about right results.

The Father-Mother God has provided abundantly for all. In truth, when a babe is born into the world it brings with it faculties that, once set to work consciously functioning in the omnipresent etheric substance, open up channels through which unfailing supply and support come to this one. The divine-life idea in the awakened soul is implanted in divine substance and brings forth a new being, the Son of God.

The realization of the following prayer will awaken man to the consciousness of his divine supply and support:

The idea of the one reality is quickened in me, and I am alive and athrill with the one radiant substance of Spirit.

Sometimes in demonstrating prosperity God's mill seemingly grinds slow. The reason is, first, that man's consciousness is functioning in such a thick envelope of materiality that it is hard to get action. And secondly, man has not yet unfolded the working power of the word.

To overcome this condition man must enter the silence and realize a prayer like this:

I am free from the clutches of inert matter. The working power of the word is quickened in me, and I understand the law governing God's abundance.

Then it is well to clinch the matter with this realization:

Divine substance flows in all its fullness into my consciousness and through me as prosperity into all my affairs.

God made us, and there is a vital connection between us and God. Keeping this truth in mind makes demonstration easy and enjoyable.

> *Be ye builders, vital, doing,*
>   *Architects of life and fate,*
> *Ever striving and preparing*
>   *For a higher, nobler state,*
> *Not in sighing, aging, dying,*
>   *Is the measure of the man,*
> *But in growing, building, living*
>   *Life fulfills the Master plan.*

Joyous Prayer

➤➤《《《

THERE are vibrations in space that our men of science have not yet discerned or measured. These undiscovered quantities are related to the Mind of Being and must be apprehended through the unfolding in man of supermind faculties. When the trained Christian metaphysician prays he can, with a disciplined consciousness, make contact with these forces in the ether and through them gain a certain unity with the Mind of Being. The consciousness thus attained is usually designated as the Christ consciousness or the mind of the Lord Jesus Christ. When the union is attained an increase in spiritual power is felt and one has the assurance of the activity of spiritual principles within of which one has had hitherto no awareness.

But no man yet knows all of life's joys, nor will he until he has come into the full understanding of spiritual communion with God. No man knows the fullness of life, nor its joys, until he has prayed in meekness and thanksgiving and has received the sweet, pure realizations of Jesus Christ. True and lasting joy arises from within. The nature of the deep inner life is revealed only to those who spiritually penetrate into its source.

Would you feed the soul on the joys of the scien-

43

tific Christian? If you would you must realize them
and give thanks in prayer for the more abundant
life. Then you will find that a great subconscious
well of living water will begin to bubble up in your
soul, and you will come to know that hitherto you
have been living in the shallows of life instead of
in its mighty depths. You will be blessed with a
knowledge of the unity of all things, and a great
peace and harmony will well up within.

Man must know spiritual harmony, and therein
is the source of a great secret. Musical geniuses
say that they first hear their compositions before
they are given outer form. Poets clothe in words
and give local habitation and a name to what to the
practical mind seems airy nothings.

Pythagoras, the ancient philosopher, wrote that
God was singing the universe into expression and
that the suns and planets were the musical notes on
a grand universal staff. Shakespeare in "The Mer-
chant of Venice" had one of his characters say:

"How sweet the moonlight sleeps upon this bank!
 Here will we sit, and let the sounds of music
 Creep in our ears: soft stillness and the night
 Become the touches of sweet harmony.
 Sit, Jessica. Look how the floor of heaven
 Is thick inlaid with patines of bright gold:
 There's not the smallest orb which thou behold'st
 But in his motion like an angel sings,
 Still quiring to the young-eyed cherubins;
 Such harmony is in immortal souls;

But whilst this muddy vesture of decay
Doth grossly close it in, we cannot hear it."

The realization of God as a great wooing, all-knowing presence, an everywhere present sustaining strength, wherein each man functions and works out his own salvation is to be established in a mighty stronghold that fortifies us against all adverse beliefs.

It is said that on the ocean of life a joyful man makes a good sailor. This is true. The strong, joyful nature will make its way where others fall by the wayside. Joy, spiritual joy, is ours by divine right, and buoys us up and urges us onward to accomplishment.

It is impossible to found a lasting stronghold within on anything less than the understanding that God is a God of joy. It is through our realization of this truth that we drink heartily of the wine of life. Often even during serene, yes, sober moments, the inner man, the inner woman, is athrill with some newborn, joyful anticipation. In prayer every high realization that comes to us is to strengthen us for greater achievements.

And when we pray, let us pray with a purpose. Purpose gives life a real meaning. Purpose gives joy and zest to living. When our eye is on the goal we are not so easily perturbed. Purpose awakens new trains of thought; purpose directs these trains of thought into new fields of achievement. Really to succeed we must have some great purpose in mind, some goal toward which we are to work. But above all, we must always purpose in our heart to achieve spiritually.

As we study the one great Presence and Power, we come to know that there is no chapter in our life that is such a failure but has back of it a grand purpose, which purpose must eventually somewhere, somehow work itself out in a most ennobling manner, well pleasing in the sight of God.

How to Handle the Psychic Forces of Consciousness

><<<

THE FIRST step of a Truth student in handling the psychic forces of consciousness is the same as that in handling any other, and that is to realize that God is the one and only power; to declare with Byron: "There is no god but God!—to prayer—lo! God is great!"

The name *psyche,* which figures in Greek mythology, means breath, life. Psyche is represented as one of the three daughters of a king. These three "daughters" are spirit, soul, and body. Psyche is the soul in its many earthly experiences, in its failures and its successes.

God is the same yesterday, today, and forever, and His law is for the use of all alike. Man interprets His law and operates in accord with it to the best of his ability in his endeavor to grow and prove his mastery over the many events that take place in his life.

If man would become expert in handling scientifically the psychical forces, he should first get a thorough understanding of just what these forces are, and above all he should know that like other forces they are subservient to God's law. The psychic

or soul realm includes the sum total of consciousness, all that the individual has experienced.

In analyzing the soul realm we have first the
animal soul. The animal soul comprises all sensa-
tions and all thoughts that we entertain with reference to animal life. Through man's thought the
animal soul forms the animal man.

The second element in the soul realm, the human
soul, is one step higher than the animal, and comprises all the thoughts and emotions we entertain
on the human plane of consciousness: thoughts of
family, of friends, of business associates, or personal possessions.

The third and highest element of soul is the spiritual. This phase of the soul is the depository of all
thoughts and aspirations we have ever had about
God and things spiritual. Here also we find a consciousness that relates us to God and forms the connecting link between the human and the divine.
When through prayers, meditations, and good works
man has built spiritual qualities into his soul to the
point of dominance over the animal and human
natures, he is ready for the regeneration with Jesus
Christ.

It is true that through the animal and human
departments of the soul we are in sympathy with
all nature, which includes the earth, the sun, the
moon, and the stars, and as these are all ensouled,
their reactions affect us when there is no higher
power in evidence. But there is a higher power in us
every one: Spirit. In Genesis it is stated that spir-

itual man, the image-and-likeness man, was given dominion over all creation. As Shakespeare aptly says,

> "The fault is not in our stars,
> But in ourselves, that we are underlings."

In our ongoing we endeavor always to bear in mind that God is the one and only power. We must know and realize that the great intelligence of God works in every conceivable way to lead us into the light, thus aiding us in avoiding error conditions. The indwelling Christ will "neither slumber nor sleep"; with the Holy Spirit it is teaching us the great truth that we are "Gods in the making" and that as such we have dominion over every thought and condition.

When Jesus was born in the manger in Bethlehem the star appeared in the east and pointed the way for the Wise Men to the spot where the young child lay. A mighty soul had been incarnated and had come to do a mighty work on the earth. So great was the occasion that the whole heavenly universe sang with joy. This to the individual means that a speck of light shone in the east, the within, revealing to the illumined soul what was taking place. The star is a symbol of potentiality; it represents expanding possibilities. The saving I AM had at last made its spiritual power manifest in the earth. But was the star seen by those who were not spiritually illumined? No. They had eyes but saw not. Only the illumined, the awakened, could per-

ceive the star of Bethlehem. So the spiritual I **AM**
is often doing a great work in a man, and the
man knows it not. This scripture also reveals the
way in which Spirit often uses the so-called psychic
to do its bidding, to reveal its power.

Today men are breaking into the psychic realm
as never before and, not being consciously unified
with Spirit, are becoming entangled in their own
mentality, in addition to the psychic vibrations of
the whole race. Often this leads to very unpleasant
experiences.

In fact all people are being quickened, and in
the absence of an understanding of Truth erratic
states of mind are formed that cause fantastic
notions about many things. Persons in this condition often become supersensitive and imagine that
they are being criticized, that others are talking about
them, and a thousand and one other things. Very
often this condition is the result of trying to communicate with the dead through mediums and spir-
itualistic seances.

There is a realm in which the souls that have left
the body are functioning feebly. Spiritualists call it
"spirit land" or "the home of the soul." The early
Christians taught that those who had passed away
were asleep. This is not true of all persons, but
those who have lived a long, strenuous life and
are weary want rest and fall asleep. Paul said, "Because you have not discerned the Lord's body you
have fallen asleep." Others who have lost their
body early in life are ready for immediate action

in reincarnation and do not find sleep necessary.

Eventually all souls reincarnate on the earth as babes and in due time take up their problems where they left off at death. But before they do reincarnate they sometimes try to communicate with their loved ones here on earth. This is never satisfactory and leads nowhere. Persons who sit in seances are taking a great risk. Instead of really getting in touch with their loved ones they are apt to make contact with psychic forces of a low order that tend to weaken their faith in God.

Paul said, "Our wrestling is not against flesh and blood, but against the principalities, against the powers, against the world-rulers of this darkness, against the spiritual *hosts* of wickedness in the heavenly *places*."

When a person is established in the Christ power and dominion, he finds that Spirit often uses the mental realm to reveal to him some message that is of vital importance to him. Such messages are imparted through dreams and visions. When the soul is still, as in sleep, the Spirit of truth throws the message on the screen of the mind in the form of thought pictures. One only has to read the symbols in order to receive the message. If the message is constructive, it is well to praise God and give thanks. If it is of a destructive nature, take the message into the silence and place it before God. Hold the thought for light until you have the realization that the illumination of Spirit permeates and penetrates the whole condition. Spiritual light transforms, re-

constructs, and makes beautiful. Joseph, the son of
Jacob, was an expert at interpreting dreams and
visions. However many of the patriarchs of old were
well versed in the art of deciphering the visions of
the night.

Again the psychic realm is the realm in which
primitive man (Adam and Eve) first functioned.
Instead of listening to the Lord they listened to the
serpent (the sense man) and learned to indulge in
sensation until it depleted divine substance. Disin-
tegration of the body followed. This is physical
death. For this cause the human family lost their
original estate in the ethereal or heavenly kingdom
and descended into earthly fleshly consciousness.

We are now, through Christ, listening to Jehovah
God, through whom we are learning the law of
life, and we are being restored to the understanding
that all the factors that enter into life are here all
the time and are ours to use. Through Christ man
has dominion. Through Christ it is possible for
us to make the perfect union between soul and body,
and enter into the consciousness of Almightiness,
thus being restored to the paradise of God from
which we originally came forth.

We should not think of the psychic realm as evil
or be afraid of it. Through Christ we possess mastery
and dominion over all realms. Through our own
Christ dominion we develop spiritual powers to
handle the psychic realm to great advantage. And
that this is a realm in which tremendous forces are
present is being discovered by the investigations of

physical science. Jesus often referred to the "kingdom of the heavens" or the kingdom of God, which
He said was very nigh unto us and even within
us. This kingdom is above the psychic, awaiting
our appropriation of it through prayer. Jesus told
His followers that after His ascension they were
to go into the upper room in Jerusalem (a high,
peaceful state of consciousness), where the Holy
Spirit would come upon them with power. Science
says the ether possesses dynamic power beyond anything we can imagine. Sir Oliver Lodge is quoted
as saying that there is energy enough in one cubic
inch of ether to run a forty-horsepower engine
for forty millions of years. This is beyond all human conception; but many of the stories that science is telling us about the power of the ether are
fully equal to this, and if they were in the Bible
skeptics would point to them as examples of the
credulity of the Christians.

Jesus says that all power should be given to us,
which carries with it the idea of unlimited capacity.

For mastery and dominion over all conditions
affirm:

I AM THAT I AM.

*Through Jesus Christ I am the master of
every realm of consciousness in my being.*

*Through Jesus Christ I enter into a full and
complete understanding of how to handle all
states of consciousness to the glory of God.*

I am illumined with the light of Spirit, and I bring "every thought into captivity to the obedience of Christ."

I commit all my works unto Jehovah, and my purposes are established.

Every plane of consciousness in me is transformed by the renewing of the mind.

Spiritual Unfoldment Makes Man Master

→»«←

ACCORDING to Genesis, Elohim God planned that man, created in His image and likeness, should have all the qualities of his Maker. At first glance this man created in the beginning seems the equal of God man or God son.

Further insight into the creative process however reveals that man has a work to do in developing his innate abilities, the "image" and "likeness." Following the paragraph "Let us make man in our image, after our likeness" we read: "And let them have dominion over the fish of the sea, and over the birds of the heavens, and over the cattle, and over all the earth, and over every creeping thing that creepeth upon the earth. And God created man in his own image, in the image of God created he him, male and female created he them. And God blessed them: and God said unto them, Be fruitful, and multiply, and replenish the earth, and subdue it; and have dominion over the fish of the sea, and over the birds . . . and over every living thing."

In modern language we would say that God imaged a man like Himself who would fulfill the law of his being when he had gained the mastery

over certain forces in his field of activity. These
forces are symbolically described as "birds," "fish,"
"cattle," and "creeping things," through which man
replenishes the earth.

The whole Bible tells of man's experience in
striving for the mastery. In addition to the Bible,
all the history of man is a record of how the human
family has struggled to fulfill the creative ideas
implanted in it from the beginning. The "birds
of the heavens" are their high ideals, the "cattle"
or "beasts of the field" are of a low order, the "fish
of the sea" are their generated or accumulated im-
pulses, and the "creeping things" represent the
micro-organisms of modern science that are claimed
to be the cause of most diseases. It has been assumed that man's dominion was to be exercised
through aggression, through physical mastery. This
idea has instigated man to wage war and rule by
tyranny, all of which his higher thoughts tell him
is in direct violation of divine law.

Our higher reason, backed by experience, forces
us to look to another source than the physical for a
solution of the problem of "dominion."

As the great example of one who became a master through spiritual unfoldment we point to Jesus,
who became the Master of all masters. Jesus was
God manifest in the flesh.

Today Jesus Christ is the realized, ideal Master.
He is the full, perfect expression of the superman.
In Him "dwelleth all the fulness of the Godhead
bodily." To Jesus Christ God was a being of infinite

goodness that He was to realize and express. So today through Jesus Christ God is a being of infinite goodness that we are to realize and express. Today the name Jesus Christ is called "Wonderful, Counsellor, Mighty God, Everlasting Father, Prince of Peace." Jesus Christ is the Master, majestic yet simple. His relation to man makes His tenderness toward humanity exquisitely touching. When we think of the mighty revolution that has taken place in the consciousness of the race through His teaching, we realize at least to a degree what He has done for the race.

"He that is slow to anger is better than the mighty;
  And he that ruleth his spirit, than he that taketh a
      city."

Jesus ruled His own spirit. Through Christ we are learning to rule our own spirits, to gain the mastery over every word and thought, yes, over every impulse of the whole being, not only on the soul plane but on the physical plane as well. His presence right in our midst is teaching us control. His presence right in our midst inspires us with new ideas, incites us to go forward to achieve.

In the world of affairs a master is one who can enforce obedience, but the Master of masters did not "enforce." Through His spiritual ability He inspired obedience.

Jesus attained mastery over sin, sickness, death. He attained a permanent state of consciousness where mortal weakness cannot enter. Emerson says

that the measure of a master is his ability to bring
all men around to his opinion within twenty years.
Today, as never before, two thousand years after
Jesus closed His ministry here on earth, He is bringing men around to His opinion or rather to His
truths as never before.

But Christ is also a servant. We follow Him because He serves best; because He bears with us
as we strive to overcome our sins—He bears our
sins with gentleness and patience. As we work in
prayer with Him, He leads us into a high state of
spiritual consciousness where we realize the allness
of God and His laws.

When Jesus was asked by a crafty lawyer to name
the greatest commandment He quickly answered that
all the Law and the Prophets could be summarized
thus: "Thou shalt love the Lord thy God with all
thy heart, and with all thy soul, and with all thy
mind. This is the great and first commandment. And
a second like *unto it* is this, Thou shalt love thy
neighbor as thyself. On these two commandments
the whole law hangeth, and the prophets." This is
a test, a challenge, to all those who would unfold
spiritually. This attitude of mind brings us in tune
with Divine Mind so that we are prepared to receive its blessings. When our thoughts are established in love, a divine synchronization takes place.
Divine Mind has a fixed rate of vibration to which,
through Christ, the mind of man is synchronized,
just as a radio receiving set is synchronized to the
frequency of a broadcasting station. In order to

tap Divine Mind we must bring the rate of vibration of our mind up to the standard, for it is only when our mind is vibrating at its most accelerated rate that God can make Himself known to us. The efficiency of the radio receiving set depends upon the number of its tubes and their adjustment to the electromagnetic field in which its kilocycles function. By this same law the perfect man must have his twelve great powers developed, operating in perfect tune with Divine Mind, in order to bring forth the image and likeness man.

In the silence when his mind is fixed steadily on God and is functioning in the consciousness of infinite love, the activities of man's brain cells synchronize with those of the very brain cells of the Master. Even the intelligent principle of the love center responds, and thus man becomes a spiritual radio with power to receive radiations from Divine Mind as well as power to broadcast them throughout his whole organism. He even is able to broadcast them throughout his environment near and far, an ability that is limited only by the spiritual power he has developed.

Humanity must bear in mind that it is traveling the road of spiritual unfoldment and hold its eye on the goal. Right here in our midst, in the mind realm as well as in the manifest world, will be developed a mighty neutralizing power that will render all destructive powers null and void, that will dissolve disease, and resurrect the consciousness of peace, health, and abundance.

Fulfillment

->>><<-

"AND GOD created man in his own image, in the image of God created he him; male and female created he them. And God blessed them." "And on the seventh day God finished his work which he had made; and he rested on the seventh day from all his work which he had made. And God blessed the seventh day, and hallowed it; because that in it he rested from all his work which God had created and made."

Science tells us that all living forms are made up of aggregations of cells, that all cells are made up of molecules and atoms, and that atoms have within them electrons and protons, the soul of light and energy, the source of everything the atom and its aggregations manifest. So we are safe in asserting that the atom at its core is Spirit and that Bible characters had this primal source of light in mind when they spoke of the light of the Spirit. Jesus proclaimed: "I am the light of the world." "Ye are the light of the world." When He spoke thus He was speaking of this inner light which gives life and intelligence to all creation. When the apostle James wrote, "Every good gift and every perfect gift is from above, coming down from the Father of lights," he was corroborating the Gospel of

John, which in the very first chapter says: "In him was life; and the life was the light of men. And the light shineth in the darkness; and the darkness apprehended it not. There came a man, sent from God, whose name was John. The same came for witness, that he might bear witness of the light, that all might believe through him. He was not the light, but came that he might bear witness of the light. There was the true light, even the light which lighteth every man, coming into the world."

These light and energy units radiate light and generate light, of which an incandescent electrical bulb is an example. From this we get a clue as to the status of man and his body as a light center with an aggregation of billions and trillions of cells, every one of them flashing light of varying color and brilliancy and forming about the body an aura of splendor. As stated in John, this aura shines in the darkness and the darkness apprehends it not. The mind must be illumined by Christ before it can behold the light radiating from every soul. When that light is developed it is visible to those who know how to still the outer mind and enter into the silence. In the 1st chapter of Revelation John says: "I was in the Spirit on the Lord's day, and I heard behind me a great voice, as of a trumpet. . . . I saw seven golden candlesticks; and in the midst of the candlesticks one like unto a son of man, clothed with a garment down to the foot, and girt about at the breasts with a golden girdle. And his head and his hair were white as white wool, *white* as snow;

and his eyes were as a flame of fire; and his feet like
unto burnished brass, as if it had been refined in
a furnace; and his voice as the voice of many waters.
. . . and his countenance was as the sun shineth in
his strength. And when I saw him, I fell at his feet
as one dead. And he laid his right hand upon me,
saying, Fear not; I am the first and the last, and
the Living one; and I was dead, and behold, I am
alive for evermore, and I have the keys of death and
of Hades."

Here John, resting at the light center of his soul,
saw the resurrected Master.

The development of this spiritual light is the
destiny of us all; and we shall not be satisfied until
we "awake in his likeness." All are radiant in a
certain degree with this spiritual light, but especially
those who have an understanding of Spirit and its
universality. We feel the light and sometimes mentally see it flashing into expression when we have
a spiritual uplift gained from a new idea of Truth.
Others feel its influence and are moved to higher
things by it; or if it is radiating gloomily, they are
moved to depression and discouragement.

The scientific understanding of the great Bible
truths thrills the soul with the desire for spiritual
attainment, with a longing for spiritual fulfillment.
Today many enlightened persons are proudly ac-
knowledging Jesus Christ as the grand and perfect
fulfillment, as perceived by John in Revelation, and
they are claiming His promises: "If ye abide in me,
and my words abide in you, ask whatsoever ye will,

and it shall be done unto you." "If a man keep my word, he shall never see death."

We revel in just concentrating upon the name Jesus Christ and in speculating about the history of His soul's unfoldment. We take delight in speculating about the true reason why He is so far in advance of our time. Surely Jesus Christ was the product of a cycle of human development that was before our present cycle of development. When here on earth, through the mastery of spiritual laws of which we today have only an inkling, He performed many seeming miracles. Think of the condition in those times of a body that had been dead for four days. Imagine Jesus thanking God that His petition had been heard and then speaking the word of life to one who had lain in the grave for this length of time. Then imagine this person instantly being charged with new life; imagine great streams of life flowing through his every cell and fiber until he came walking out of the tomb, restored to perfect health. Imagine Jesus in the consciousness of perfect unity with God speaking the healing word to many "sick unto death" and each one instantly throwing off the disease and coming forward sound and well.

Jesus taught us how to pray. He taught us that prayer is not only the spiritual approach to the Father but that through prayer and realization we attain the interpenetrating consciousness of God's perfect life and love and power. Jesus revealed to us that we are the sheep of His pasture; that is,

that we are children of the same Father as He. He
is our Elder Brother, our helper. We are His people, and He is interested in our progress.

Jesus Christ has provided and provides today the
greatest impetus to the ongoing of our race. When
the soul of the race (symbolized by Eve) became
involved in the pleasures of sensation (symbolized
by the serpent) and sought other guidance than
that of Jehovah God, gradual degeneration of the
whole human family began until men were in a
bad way. Something had to be done. Someway,
somehow we had to be lifted out of the murky
darkness of sense thought.

To lift the race out of sense thought Jesus was
compelled by the necessity of soul sympathy to become an intimate associate of the people He sought
to help. Hence He incarnated into the race and was
"tempted in all points as we are, but without sin."

Through His experience on the cross, where His
precious blood was spilled, through His suffering
there Jesus lowered His consciousness to the consciousness of the race, thereby administering to the
whole race a blood transfusion, imparting to both
the soul and the body of men the properties of Being that will restore man to his divine estate.

With their blood transfusions the medical men
of today are copying this grand transfusion of life.
We are on the way to fulfillment and the Jesus
Christ way!

Jesus Christ broadcast the electrons of His blood
into the race thought atmosphere, and they may be

apprehended by all who believe in Him. These electrons become centers of energy and life in those who appropriate them, and thus men gradually transform and regenerate their blood and their body. This is the real spiritual meaning of being saved by Jesus Christ.

The blood is the life. Jesus really came to bring to the whole human family a larger consciousness of life. He said, "I came that ye may have life, and may have it more abundantly."

Life is a universal energy that moves even the corpuscles of the blood. Therefore life is more powerful than the blood. Consequently we believe that it was through the "shedding," the getting rid, of the idea of flesh and blood that Jesus accomplished His great works. He tapped the great reservoir of divine life and raised His consciousness of life to that of the Father. Through Him we all have access to this perpetual life stream. We must really eat of His substance, as He taught us; that is, we must appropriate it as spiritually ours. We must drink of His blood: let His life stream flow through our mind and body, healing, cleansing, and purifying us in every way. This is the grand at-one-ment (atonement) of man's life with the life of God through Jesus Christ. This is the way to perfect fulfillment.

Unfoldment

->>><<<-

God's pure life and substance are constantly
renewing and rebuilding His holy temple,
my body.

New and rich ideas arise in my mind, and I
demonstrate prosperity.

->>><<<-

"UNITY claims that the Bible teaches evolution; just where is the evolution of Jesus
taught?"

The evolution of Jesus was a combination of
mind and body unfoldment.

The body of Jesus developed from germs planted
in Mary, His mother. Science says that all stages of
unfoldment from the most primitive animal to man
are illustrated in the development of the human
organism. So we must conclude that the body of
Jesus was an unfoldment from sense to Spirit.

However Unity teaches the evolution of both
soul and body; an evolution summarized in the 1st
chapter of John under the head of the unfoldment
of the Word. Bible authorities say that "Word" is
a poor translation of the Greek word *Logos. Logos*

conveys the idea of implanted God—Mind in man—
from which the perfect man logically evolves.

God is Spirit. In creation Spirit takes the form
of mind, implanting itself in substance and becoming manifest as perfect man. Here is condensed
in a few words what would take volumes to describe. Here are epitomized all books on physiology
and evolution, mental science and psychology, religion and spiritual philosophy.

In the rocks beneath our feet are preserved the
bones of mammoth creatures that have been suc-
ceeded by finer types of animal life. Here is evidence of evolution from lower to higher types of
life. Anthropology teaches that the earth has been
inhabited by man for at least half a million years.
Many hold that the present body of man has within
it natural forces that would transform it if they
were released. Those who read between the lines
have discovered that the Bible veils evolution in
rites, ceremonies, and acts of personalities.

As all words in every language have their root
in the thoughts and acts of man, so all the rites and
ceremonies of religion represent man's relation to
his source, God, and the development of his soul.

The two baptisms, that of John and Jesus, represent the two common steps in the growth of the soul,
denial and affirmation, the dropping of the old and
the laying hold of the new. This is evolution.

In totality John the Baptist represents the per-
fected natural man who recognizes his finality and
his willingness to surrender his personality so that

the superman Christ may supplant him, thus symbolizing the evolution of the soul from the personal
to the spiritual.

It is essential that a clear understanding be had
of the principles involved in the transition from the
natural to the spiritual, otherwise the way will be
difficult.

Jesus praised John as the most perfect of those
born of women—that is, of the Adam or natural
man—but He explained that John even in his perfection was not to be compared with the spiritual
man. He also commented on the futile efforts of
those on the natural plane who attempt by will
force (violence) to attain the spiritual ("kingdom
of heaven").

In the process of developing out of the natural
into the spiritual not only the mind but the body
also is affected. The energy locked up in the cells
of the physical are released and the body of flesh
is transformed into a radiant body of light. This is
a day-by-day transformation of the cells until the
whole body is "electrified" and passes over into the
fourth dimension or kingdom of the heavens. Jesus
accomplished this transformation of His body and it
became an electrical dynamo broadcasting life germs
through our race consciousness. We are to follow
Him in this transformation.

These life germs of Jesus' body form the nucleus
of a new race organism for all people. All persons
everywhere may partake of (eat) the radiant body
(bread) of Jesus by exercising faith in Him as the

great source of pure Spirit substance, sown as soul seed for the saving of humanity from sense consciousness.

Not only may one eat of this superbody substance but one may also drink through faith of His transcendent life. Such eating of His body and drinking of His life or blood is the "Holy Communion" of which sincere Christians partake daily.

The understanding that this very intimate relation exists between Jesus and His true followers is transforming the body of thousands of Christians who formerly labored under the thought that the new body in Christ was to be attained after death.

"I am the resurrection, and the life." "If a man keep my word, he shall never see death."

When man understands that he is always right in the presence of a supermind force that is perpetually pushing him into higher states of consciousness and finer physical radiations, he cannot help co-operating with it in the divine urge toward higher things.

No man can retard this universal upward sweep of the whole creation, but in the exercise of his inherent free will man can insulate his soul and body, separate himself from it, and thus become lost in the delusions of sense. To join the Holy Spirit in its efforts to gain the attention and co-operation of all men we make it a practice to join with people of like mind in every walk of life in affirming words that bind us to the mighty moving Spirit of Jesus Christ.

Thought Images

I see myself as God sees me, perfect in mind
and body.

What I image in mind is molded in omnipresent substance, and I behold plenty for
everybody.

EVERY TIME we go to a movie we are witness-
ing a likeness of what is constantly taking
place in our mind. A likeness is an imita-
tion or repetition of a thing. The projection into
visible action of a series of small images by a motion-
picture machine is the copy of a process that we all
use, the picture-making ability of our mind. However the picture-making ability of our mind is a far
more substantial thing than the weak imitations of
the movie camera. We clothe our mental pictures
with flesh and blood, while the movie is merely
shimmering shadows.

It is true that persons who are shallow in their
grasp of the deep things of life image weakly, and
the projections of their mind are transitory. But
those who have meditated seriously upon the source

70

of existence and stirred up the inner substance and life make very substantial pictures in the universal ether or "kingdom of the heavens." An image projected from the head alone, which has not made union with soul substance, is a mere flickering will-o'-the-wisp that shimmers for a short moment in the mental marshes and then fades away.

There is a vast difference between the thought images of an intellectual thinker and those of one who has got access to the spiritual substance and life within. One may make brilliant pictures in the ether, but they are without the substance and life that is so essential to the structure of things eternal. Jesus illustrated this in His comparison of the man who builds upon rock with the man who builds upon sand. The house built upon sand soon falls, but the one built on rock (substance) endures when the winds and floods descend upon it.

Spiritual insight or discernment shows us that Divine Mind, which created in the beginning, must still be carrying forward the universe and the man that it originally conceived. It also shows us that by projecting the perfect picture of ourselves that God projected we shall behold its perfect manifestation.

Paul says that we shall attain the glory of the Lord by degrees: "from glory to glory." Jesus said, "In your patience ye shall win your souls." So many of us have visions of the perfect man, as had John on Patmos, and we are so eager to be like him that we get impatient and eagerly grasp at the many "promising" short cuts into the kingdom.

But we should be constantly reminded that there are no shorter cuts than those taught by Jesus. He said that the kingdom of heaven suffered violence under John the Baptist and the other prophets up to the time of John and that the violent took it by force. Then He called attention to John the Baptist as the reincarnation of Elijah. Of all the old prophets Elijah was the most violent and destructive. He at one time called down the fire of Jehovah and destroyed four hundred of the prophets of Baal. This violent and destructive rise of the power of the word finally reacted upon the cells of Elijah's body and burned them up, and he was taken up into the heavens in a chariot of fire.

It is popularly taught that Elijah is a saint in heaven, but this cannot be true because, as Jesus plainly taught in Matthew 11:14, he appeared again in the earth as John the Baptist. Neither did John get into heaven. He expressed the Elijah spirit by condemning Herod and then having his head cut off by way of reaction to his destructive thought. All this instructs us in the power of our mind to bring peace, harmony, and health into our life by right thinking. All that Jesus taught about man and his mighty mental capacity is being confirmed by modern psychology and by the discoveries of science in the realms invisible. For us it is not only a privilege but an absolute necessity to bring forth that perfection of character and form which was originally imaged in our soul by God-Mind.

The Spoken Word

→»)«←

Spirit life quickens mind and body, and I am whole.

Spirit substance fills my mind and floods my affairs.

→»)«←

WE UNDERSTAND that the worlds were framed by the word of God spoken in faith. This in substance is the comment of the author of Hebrews. If God created by the power of His word it is fair to assume that He gave like power to man, who has in miniature all the abilities of His Father. Jesus confirmed this power of man's word when He said that we should be held accountable for our lightest word and that our words would both justify and condemn us.

Our words are so interwoven with our thoughts and acts that we do not discern the relation between cause and effect, in fact we do not as a rule see any connection between them. We are so concerned with effects that we have no consciousness of causes. So in explaining the law by which man builds his character, body, and environment, we must repeatedly call attention to the source of these things, Spirit and its outlet in man, the word. Thought and word are so intimately allied that we usually count them as one. "Out of the abundance of the heart the mouth speaketh." Get a deep conviction of the truth of your cause; then speak it forth in strong words, and it will surely come to pass.

The process through which the idea—conceived in mind, formed in thought, and made manifest in body and affairs—passes in its various stages is not always clear, and we are not usually concerned about the manner in which the end is accomplished. The fulfillment of our objective is the principal thing.

However it is within the province of man to understand and witness the whole process of creative thought in his own organism. It requires soul culture of an advanced order to do this, and but few persons are willing to undertake the necessary study and discipline. It is not taught in any of the metaphysical schools, because the instructions cannot be put in words. No words have yet been invented to express the attitudes of mind and body required to raise the cell life in man's body to the required potency. The spiritual ether in which we float has a rate of vibration millions of times greater than matter. This is the kingdom of Spirit life, which Jesus brought to our attention and of which we must lay hold if we would attain eternal or continuous life. The individuality or I AM must give concentrated attention to this inner life energy and introduce it into mind and body continually until the whole nervous system is aflame with Spirit life. We may not be conscious of it, but we are all seeking this inner life flame, because its energy is the only source upon which we can draw to raise our atomic vibration to the point where it will overcome the slow disintegrating flow of human nature.

There are souls in the heavens who have accomplished this and so attuned their bodies to the spiritual life that they are no longer subject to death. Jesus of Nazareth is the illumined soul appointed to save our race from the disintegrating effects of broken law, and through Him we are dynamically infused with life.

Every time we listen to a radio program we have in the diffusion of intelligence an illustration of what Jesus accomplished in the diffusion of life. In the 1st chapter of John we read, "In him was life; and the life was the light of men."

Here light (intelligence) and life are treated as one. Like all the attributes of Spirit, intelligence or the knowing quality is united with the active quality, life. There is a spiritual ether corresponding to the radio ether, into which Jesus merged His soul and body at His disappearance in the heavens *(hoi ouranoi)*. Here awaiting our appropriation is a radiant intelligence and life. When we turn our attention within and give ourselves up wholly to Spirit, we are quickened with a life and intelligence of superexcellence.

When the blood stream becomes depleted our

physicians hasten to make a blood transfusion, overlooking the fact that Jesus made it possible for all of us to receive from Him a life transfusion that not only revives us in temporal ills but, above all, begins in our body a purifying and energizing process that will finally save us from death.

When we strive to be like Jesus in thought and word we are quickened by Him and are lifted up. This results in healing; but far more important, we are inoculated with the germs of soul and body cleansing.

Thou Shalt Decree

→»«←

In the presence and power of the Christ in me
I decree the manifestation of perfect health.

In the presence and power of the living
Christ substance I claim the riches of God.

→»«←

GOD MADE man by the power of His word:
"God said, Let us make man in our image,
after our likeness." By virtue of his spiritual
origin and the power vested in him man forms by
his word the world in which he lives. Jehovah said
to Eliphaz, "Thou shalt also decree a thing, and it
shall be established unto thee."

Every word man utters energizes the ether with
a creative impulse that in due season brings forth its
image and likeness.

The formative power of man's thought and word
is governed by his faith in himself and the vehe-
mence with which he thinks and speaks.

Jesus expected great things of His followers because He knew what is in man. He knew that man
has laid hold of the power of God, as stated in
Genesis 3:22, "Behold, the man is become as one

of us." Jesus recognized this when He said, "Is it
not written in your law, I said, Ye are gods?"

We have not brought forth in the majesty of
the sons of God because of our self-depreciation
and our ignorance of the creative law implanted
in us. Job had the inferiority complex of personality. He whined:

"Behold, I am of small account; what shall I an-
        swer thee? . . .
    Then Jehovah answered Job out of the whirlwind,
        and said,
    Gird up thy loins now like a man:
    I will demand of thee, and declare thou unto me . . .
    Deck thyself now with excellency and dignity;
    And array thyself with honor and majesty."

Isaiah said, "Woe unto them that decree unrighteous decrees." Our woes can be traced right
back to some unrighteous decree. We have decreed
a thousand things that we did not want to come to
pass, but that have come to pass, and we are suffering the woeful consequences.

Our body is weak or strong, according to what
we have decreed for it. Every organ is functioning as we have decreed. If we have said, "My
stomach is weak,"' the obedient life and substance
have found this kind of stomach for us. If we have
declared strength and vigor for our stomach, this
organ will at once begin to carry out our decree.
"Say the word, and my servant shall be healed."

So every organ and member of the body responds to our decree.

Man is the anointed son of God called Christ. When we know the truth about ourselves we are freed from the bondage of the foolish decrees of personality. Do not exalt personality in your decrees for yourself. Exalt Christ by making your decrees in His name. "Christ in you, the hope of glory."

The vital energy of eternal life exists in every cell of our body. Science proclaims that its experiments with animal tissues prove that man's body would live forever if it were not for his brain. In a recent interview Doctor Carrel says that "the only thing that keeps men from living forever is the possession of a brain and nervous system."

Metaphysicians know that the brain and nervous system are the organ of the mind, and that man dies because he is not wise in his directive power.

"And the Almighty will be thy treasure,
    And precious silver unto thee"
was the prosperity proclamation of our wise old friend Job.

A "depression" took everything he owned, even his sons and daughters. But he was not defeated, he claimed his own and it was restored to him:
"Hear, I beseech thee, and I will speak;
 I will demand of thee, and declare thou unto me . . .
 And Jehovah gave Job twice as much as he had
    before."

Be Strong in the Lord

→»»«←

I praise and give thanks that I am strong in
the Lord and in the power of His might.

I praise and give thanks for the plenty,
visible and invisible, that I feel and see
everywhere.

→»»«←

TO BE "strong in the Lord, and in the power
of his might" means that we are seeking
strength and power from sources other than
the physical. Food and exercises are the usual sources
of bodily vigor. We are not discussing mental vigor,
which is gained by combining diet, discipline, and
idealism.

A study of Truth reveals that words based upon
the authority of Spirit develop dynamic force. The
difference between the force of a word based in
physical things and one based in spiritual things is
the difference between the effect one gets from contact with a wire carrying a light and a wire carrying
a heavy voltage.

The time will come when scientific metaphysics
will measure mathematically the currents of energy

80

emanating from a brain charged with material ideas and one charged with spiritual ideas. At present the science of mind is quite primitive. We are, like Franklin, flying a few kites and making cursory excursions into a field of energy the control of which will eventually change our whole world.

We have found however that very definite changes occur in our mind and body when we practice concentration in the silence. This means that when we want to gain spiritual power we get still mentally and physically and turn our attention within. On our first entering this "silence" we close our eyes and ears, and with our concentrated attention fixed on an imaginary point within, we repeat silently any set of words that carry a spiritual idea. With practice we can make the inner connection without closing the eyes.

In His directions for effective prayer Jesus told His disciples to go into the secret place and close the door, there to pray to the Father in secret, and the response would appear outwardly. Jesus sometimes prayed all night. He taught persistence in prayer. We find that contact with the supermind—which Jesus named the Father—is sometimes quickly made in concentrated prayer; then again our mind is slow to see the inner light. The relation of our mind to creative Mind may be compared to the relation of a radio receiving set to a broadcasting station. As we must tune our radio set so that it will pick up waves from the proper station, so we have to acquire the ability to attune our mind to Divine

Mind, so we may learn by spiritual understanding the true ideas that exist eternally in Divine Mind.

Every word has a quality that sympathetically relates it to an idea innate in the mind of man, and when the word is released it radiates an energy that contracts or expands the body cells and through them external nature. For example, words of praise, gratitude, or thanksgiving expand, set free, and in every way radiate energy. Words of failure or impotence congest energy and cause the cells to crowd together, making nerves trembly and bones brittle.

When the thoughts are lifted up to the contemplation of our all-pervading and all-powerful Spirit Father and our voices ring out in words of praise and thanksgiving, the withered hands and shackled feet are freed, the walls of negation are shattered, and we step forth into a new consciousness of life.

To those in the clutches of adverse words it seems a travesty to praise and give thanks to the God of strength and power, but thousands of those who have endured poverty and sickness for years find that their prison doors open when they praise and give thanks, like Paul and Silas, as related in the 16th chapter of Acts. They were praying and singing hymns to God when suddenly there was a great earthquake, all the prisoners' chains were loosened, and Paul and Silas stepped forth free men.

So you will find that you can be freed from all the prison cells of mind's blind thinking by lifting up your voice and heart in songs of praise and thanksgiving to the God of freedom, light, and life.

Face to Face with God

→»«←

Thy Spirit strengthens both my soul and my body, and I rest in the peace of wholeness and health.

Every anxious thought is stilled. Thy mighty confidence and Thy peace infold me. Omnipresent Spirit substance fills my mind, and abundance is everywhere manifest.

→»«←

MANY CHRISTIAN metaphysicians who are quite familiar with the idea of the omnipresence of God address Him in terms that imply His absence. Instead of talking direct to God, who is always right in our midst, we talk about Him. We are apt to say, "God strengthens both my soul and my body" instead of "Thy Spirit strengthens both my soul and my body."

Our words betray our dominant state of mind, although the logic of Truth may belie this. We see logically that there cannot be any separation in spirit between the Creator and the created, but the created has the power to think of itself as separate from its source, and this thought makes a mental vacuum in which there is a total absence of spiritual attributes. The human family on this planet has set up this sort of a mental void, and unless we train our mind to think the truth, we find ourselves talking to God as if He were in the next room or in some faraway heaven in the skies.

We in our day and age are not alone in making God the third person in our conversation. Bible authors did the same. We should remember that the people who live today are the same people who lived in the past, in other words, we are people who thought ourselves separate from God life and thereby killed our body. We also are like some of the people who acted the part of the prodigal son, desiring to be again united with the Father.

However we should not forget that although the Father was "moved with compassion, and ran, and fell on his neck, and kissed him," the prodigal was yet "afar off." No one save Jesus has fully bridged this gulf of separation, and we are excusable if we at times lapse into the old consciousness of absence from the Father. Jesus gives us the right cue when He affirms, "It is the spirit that giveth life; the flesh profiteth nothing: the words that I have spoken unto you are spirit, and are life."

"For as the Father hath life in himself, even so gave he to the Son also to have life in himself."

We find that we must train our mind in trust, look persistently and continuously to God for all things, and rest in the assurance that what we ask and affirm in Spirit will surely come to pass. Jesus had such supreme confidence and faith in the Father as the source of health and prosperity that His name has become the synonym and open door for the manifestation of those things. He said that whatever we asked of the Father in His name would be granted. Many persons get a very definite mental uplift and consciousness of Spirit by repeating audibly and silently the name of Jesus Christ. But the name does not represent the real character of the person unless it is known to us through our acquaintance with the person himself. Unless you have read about Jesus and tried to realize His love, wisdom, and supermind power, you have no conception of the meaning of His name. Paul urged that we let Christ be formed in us. That means that through the study of the life of Jesus and the discipline He gave His mind we shall put into our mind the same ideas that He had. These ideas will form in our mind a new kind of man, which is God's man.

When you turn your attention to Spirit your mind makes contact with a realm of ideas very much above the level of your common thinking; and when you strike this mental stratosphere you are tremendously lifted up. Then you make your statements of Truth and whatever you decree comes to pass. Job's friend Eliphaz said to him:

"Acquaint now thyself with him, and be at peace:
  Thereby good shall come unto thee. . . .
  Thou shalt also decree a thing, and it shall be established unto thee;
  And light shall shine upon thy ways"

Not Magic but Law

→≫≪←

I see myself as God sees me, strong, robust,
healthy.

The Spirit of industry, energy, and honesty
now stirs me to action, and I am truly
prosperous.

→≫≪←

THERE IS AN idea quite prevalent in the public
mind that we teach a system of thought and
word juggling; that anyone anywhere can
have any and every thing by merely repeating over
and over certain magic words. It is true that words
have magic in them and very often the result of the
mental imagery evoked by them is so startling as to
suggest Aladdin and his lamp. However a comprehension of the whole philosophy reveals a well-
balanced set of principles upon which it rests. By
being determined one can project an isolated idea
and gets results without conforming to the accepted
laws of human relationships. No one can use the
dynamic power of thought and word in unbalanced
ways without suffering undesirable reactions. To
avoid this we keep before our mind's eye the dominant existence of a divine order and law to which

we must conform if we are to attain enduring success. Jesus taught that He was the executive of a spiritual principle that was the source, the wisdom, and the power of everything He did. He urged His followers to look to the same inner power. "Seek, and ye shall find; knock, and it shall be opened unto you."

We who are striving to acquire an understanding of the divine law and to apply it in our life as Jesus did in His should set up the same intimate relation with the Father that He did. "For the Father loveth the Son, and showeth him all things that he himself doeth." We are all the offspring of God and come into sonship when we acquaint ourselves with His mind.

In the beginning of our existence as free, thinking entities we had a certain consciousness of the Father-Mind, but continued thinking of ourselves as independent of this Mind has formed a gulf of apartness. We are prodigals in the far country of sense life. Those of us who are beginning to see how poor and bare this material life is have turned our faces to the Father's house and are mentally journeying home. It is not a question of geographical locality but of mental recognition. "The kingdom of God is within you," said Jesus. Seeking God within changes our whole mental viewpoint. We find ourselves right in the presence of creative Mind, and seeking to co-operate with this Mind, we receive spiritual inspiration and are guided in even the most minute details of life.

In the early stages of our spiritual awakening we realize our dependence upon God for all that we are, and our attitude is that of the humble, obedient child. Then gradually there arises within us the consciousness of sonship, the consciousness that God is the parent Mind and that we inherit all the ideas constituting this mind. If we inherit these creative ideas it logically follows that we are to use them. This is where, as Jesus explained, the son becomes the co-operator with the Father in creation. "For as the Father hath life in himself, even so gave he to the Son also to have life in himself: and he gave him authority to execute judgment, because he is a son of man." The claim that Jesus was the exclusive and only Son of God is here refuted: "because he is a son of man." By divine right man is the executive power of God-Mind, and he will never fulfill the law of his being before he enters into the realization of his dominion and authority in the realms of mind and matter.

Thus we see that we are warranted in affirming our unity with God and expecting the attributes of the perfect man to appear. "Judge not according to appearance." Right in the face of adverse appearances enter into God-Mind and see yourself as He sees you, strong, robust, healthy. Jesus said, "Marvel not at this: for the hour cometh, in which all that are in the tombs shall hear his voice, and shall come forth." All those who believe in the inevitable conquest of death are already in mental tombs, but when they realize that Jesus walked out of the tomb and said, "Follow me," they are lifted into the heavens of eternal life. Do not be afraid to go all the way with Jesus.

When the prodigal son returned, the father ran to meet him, ordered the best robe to be put upon him, shoes on his feet, a ring on his hands; and he provided a feast, with merriment. Here is parabled the prosperity that ensues when man returns to the consciousness of God as his resource. In the world of affairs, industry, energy, and honesty are expected of those who would succeed. These qualities have a divine source and can be quickened and intensely energized by attaching them to the dynamic mind of God. "Thou shalt also decree a thing, and it shall be established unto thee."

Spiritual Soul Therapy

→>X<←

I praise Thee and bless Thee for the consciousness of health and wholeness through
Christ.

With all Thy pople I praise and bless Thy
Spirit of plenty now manifest everywhere.

→>X<←

PSYCHOANALYSIS is growing more popular every
day because it measures the capacity of the
soul. We are all interested in our soul and
how to save it. Those who follow Jesus go one step
further in soul therapy than the average psychoan-
alyst; they incorporate Spirit with soul and make
it the primal source and sustainer of both soul and
body. "It is the spirit that quickeneth."

We make our soul out of the thoughts and words
we entertain. Consequently we should be very careful in choosing our words, because they are the
means by which we convey Spirit to character and
its structure. So instead of psychoanalysis let us say
we have Spirit psychoanalysis.

Every word has its root in an idea, whether this
idea is reflected from within or not. When we wish

to approve, extol, applaud, or commend we praise and bless. Words of this kind and the mental attitudes that they set up stimulate, quicken, whirl into action, and finally establish in character the ideals of which they are the vehicle. So let us remember that we use words as instruments of ideas and that it is the idea that we are seeking to enlarge and establish by our words of praise and blessing.

So "praise" and "bless" are words freely used by those who love spiritual values, because these words are heavily charged with capacity to express creative Mind. In themselves alone the words "praise" and "bless" are potent for good because they are associated with ideas that eulogize the good. These words are not found in the vocabulary of the pessimist or atheist. From various sources we learn that scientists are experimenting with instruments like the lie tester that register mind emotions. These instruments measure the force of fear and courage, sorrow and joy; in fact every emotion and mental attitude is coming under scientific observation, and it will not be long before we can produce graphs of the power of every thought as it registers on the nerve and brain cells of the body. When these brain testers definitely prove that certain emotions not only stimulate but permanently enlarge brain areas the cultivation of constructive states of mind will become part of our common-school curriculums.

Metaphysicians find that words that express thanks, gratitude, and praise release latent energies of mind and spirit; and the effects of their use fol-

low so quickly that they can almost be identified
with the originating words.

Let your words of praise and blessing be to Spirit
and the increase will be even greater than it has
been when addressed to man. The resource of Spirit
are beyond our highest flights of imagination. You
can praise a weak body into strength, a fearful heart
into peace and trust; shattered nerves into poise and
power; a failing business into prosperity and success; want and insufficiency into supply and support.

The healing and prosperity thoughts in this chapter are a guide for those who are trying to demonstrate the power of words to regulate health and
finances. If you are in need of health use the statement as printed, putting special emphasis on the
words "strength" and "power." When using these
health-producing words, direct your attention to
Spirit as if it were an interpenetrating presence,
which it is. Try to feel the quickening spiritual
harmony and health, which will be manifested at
once or later, depending on your attitude toward
the time element. If you join in thought with Silent
Unity every night from nine to ten o'clock you will
get a powerful uplift. In demonstrating prosperity
you should praise and bless even minor evidences of
financial improvement.

Remember what Jesus said about your mental attitude in demonstrating spiritually: "And all things,
whatsoever ye shall ask in prayer, believing, ye shall
receive"; which may be rephrased thus: Pray, believing that you have received, and you shall receive.

Health and Prosperity

→»×«←

My health is in Thee, and I affirm Thee and
Thy life as the one and only source of my
healing.

Thou art my resource, and in Thee I am
bountifully supplied with all things.

→»×«←

GOD IS SPIRIT, and Spirit is located and appears
wherever it is recognized by an intelligent
entity. It thus follows that whoever gives his
attention to Spirit and seals his identification with
it by his word, starts a flow of Spirit life and all
the attributes of Spirit in and through his consciousness. To the extent that he practices identify-
ing himself with the one and only source of existence he becomes Spirit, until finally the union
attains a perfection in which he can say with Jesus,
"I and the Father are one."

Many persons who have been taught that God
exists in a realm separate from His creations and
that He has parts and passions like man discount
the claim that He is the essence of man's body. But
that Spirit is the essence of all things is good logic,

and those who have made the contact with Spirit
life testify that it has revealed itself to them as the
very source of their existence; that is, as creative
Mind, God.

Jesus was undoubtedly the most radical of all the
thousands who have claimed that God revealed Himself to them right out of omnipresence.

The same thought stuff that God used to create
man is accessible to man at all times and in all
places. In fact we are using this all-potential thought
stuff with every mental concept. Thus we plant ideas
in the same soil in which God-Mind plants its ideas,
and the offspring or fruit is of the same kind. "Whatsoever a man soweth, that shall he also reap."

Following the creative law that works constantly
in Spirit substance and life, we find that we are
creating permanent thought forms when our ideals
are in harmony with divine law. We thus see that
our immortal body is formed when our thoughts
harmonize with what we intuitively know to be
God thoughts, and the perishable body is formed
when we think and speak words that are out of line
with Truth as established in divine principle.

God is Spirit. God is the source of all that we are,
hence the source of life, substance, and intelligence.
The one and only substance out of which all things
are formed is right here at all times, awaiting our
recognition of it in its spiritual freedom. When we
do recognize it in the simple faith that it will carry
out our demands, we are doing just what Jesus did.

In like manner the divine substance, out of which

all things are formed, in its spiritual freedom is here in our midst waiting for us to form it into whatever we may decree. Thus it follows that God has actually planted man in a garden or paradise of potential substance (mental soil), out of which he can grow his prosperity.

Thousands are testifying in this day that a greater work is being done in His name than was done in Palestine.

Your health and prosperity will surely be demonstrated if you are faithful in your open-mindedness; in holding fast to healing and prosperity thoughts.

Thoughts Are Things

→»>«←

I am no longer like Lot's wife, preserving
evil in mind and body by remembering it. I
relax and willingly let go of all effete substance, that the new, pure radiance of God
may be made manifest in me.

My mind no longer clings to the complexity
of mortal finances. I am open to the splendor
of the kingdom of God within, and a flood
of plenty follows.

→»>«←

ONE OF the axiomatic truths of metaphysics
is that "thoughts are things." That the mind
of man marshals its faculties and literally
makes into living entities the ideas that it entertains
is also a foregone conclusion.

The word "things" expresses poorly the active
and very vital character of the thoughts to which the
mind gives life, substance, and intelligence.

We see so many inanimate "things" around us
in the material world, and we compare our creative
thoughts with them and thereby get a very inferior

conception of the marvelous ability of our mind in its creative capacity.

Shakespeare says, "The poet's pen . . . gives to airy nothing a local habitation and a name." At the same time the poet's mind forms in the ether a replica of his idea, and that replica takes up its habitation in his thought atmosphere and henceforth injects into it a tincture of the sentiments that the poets originally had.

This ability of the Adamic man to "name" or give character, form, and shape to ideas is symbolically described in the 2d chapter of Genesis, where Jehovah God brought before Adam the elemental ideas or "beasts" of the Garden of Eden (called by metaphysicians the "ether"). "And whatsoever the man called every living creature, that was the name thereof."

We often refer in Unity literature to the discoveries by modern science of the ether and its stupendous properties as confirming in scientific terms what Jesus taught in symbols concerning the properties of the ether, which He named the kingdom of the heavens. The Garden of Eden is a symbolic description of that elemental realm which modern science has named the ether. Science says that this ether fills all space, is not molecular, and possesses an amount of energy beyond comparison with anything material; that all the complex phenomena of nature may be reduced to different kinds of waves of energy in the ether. Professor James Jeans says, "We live in a universe of waves, and

nothing but waves." He also says that it may be that
our mind lays hold of the atoms of our body and so
forms the world about us.

Here we see how very near to the teaching of
religion scientific minds are approaching. They are
virtually proclaiming the one life as the source of
everything. Their next great proclamation will be
that one directive intelligence is an essential cause
of the harmonious universe.

Every experienced metaphysician knows that
man's mind molds from an omnipresent element
whatever takes form, shape, and intelligence and becomes part of his thought world. That science in a
measure confirms this is a source of gratification and
a stabilizer of faith. Knowing that our world is composed of what we have idealized should make us
more watchful of the activities of our mind. Are we
still harboring thought forms that are impeding our
soul's progress? Are we preserving our evil thoughts
by thinking about them with fear in our mind? Or
it may be that we yearn for the pleasures of the
past and like Lot's wife look back, thereby sub-
jecting ourselves to the things of the past or with
the salt of the mind preserving them. There are
always better things just ahead for those who build
in mind the living thought entities that go before
and open the way.

Man lives in two worlds, the world of cause and
the world of effect. The world of effect is at present
in a complex tangle. Panaceas without number are
offered. There is but one panacea and that is the

installation of an economic system in which human greed will be eliminated. To institute such a system will require men and women who have overcome greed in themselves.

If you would help the world, and incidentally yourself, to better economic conditions, begin to deny your selfishness and greed and affirm,

"I am open to the splendor of the kingdom of God within, and a flood of plenty follows."

The Supermind

->))((<-

I join with all the hosts of heaven in declaring that only the good is true, and that good health everywhere is made manifest.

The rich substance of the kingdom of God is pouring its plenty perpetually into my mind and affairs, and I am in all ways prospered.

->))((<-

THAT MAN in his spiritual nature is leagued with supermind realms is taught freely in the Scriptures and can be proved to the satisfaction of anyone who will submit to the required mental discipline. That these supermind forces are not always used to bring about good is no argument against their existence. Anyone who develops spiritually in any way breaks into realms of thought energy superior to the intellectual and can incite to action subtle causes that mystify the average onlooker. For this reason every Christian metaphysician should have some acquaintance with these facts about the supermind, which occupies so great a place in Truth demonstrations.

The question is often asked if the Indian medicine man or the African witch doctor uses the same force that the Christian healer does. The answer is yes. There is but one primal life in which we all exist and which we use as we will. The way in which we project this force determines whether we are Christian or pagan. If our thought is to destroy, we are pagan. If our thought is for peace, we are Christian. This law is operative not only in the nations but in every individual. As we are taught in our Bible, God originally guided man to think good only; but man was tempted and chose to be free and think for himself. This freedom threw the whole race into a mental vortex of "good" and "evil," hate and love, war and peace. Christ is the Prince of Peace and Satan is the devil of destruction.

These good and evil states of consciousness form the heavens and the hells of the race, and we go in mind to heaven or hell every time we mentally project the thoughts that "chord" with that particular state. Only a supermastermind can overcome this law of mental affinity and set up in our earthly discordant thought atmosphere a consciousness of peace and love. Jesus was able to do this, and when we think of Him, the Christ in us "tunes in" to the Christ in Him and we are saved from the destructive forces that tear soul and body asunder.

The mental harmony of Jesus not only radiates throughout the earth but reaches into the heavens, where it taps the glory of the Son of God. When we pray in the name of the Lord Jesus Christ or decree His presence and power in our spiritual work, we effect a reunion with His supermind and its tremendous ramifications in heaven and earth, and our own meager spiritual ability is augmented a thousandfold. Jesus understood and used this law of thought affinity when He claimed that the works He did were not His but the Father's within Him. It was in this consciousness that He proclaimed, "All authority hath been given unto me in heaven and on earth." He also affirmed a like spiritual unity for His disciples and for all those who proclaim Him as their spiritual leader. His last promise was "And these signs shall accompany them that believe: in my name shall they cast out demons; they shall speak with new tongues; they shall take up serpents, and if they drink any deadly thing, it shall in no wise hurt them; they shall lay hands on the sick, and they shall recover." This is found in the 16th chapter of Mark, where it is also written, "And they went forth, and preached everywhere, the Lord working with them, and confirming the word by the signs that followed."

Peter and John developed marvelous healing power when they spoke the magic words to the lame man at the gate Beautiful: "In the name of Jesus Christ of Nazareth, walk." "And immediately his feet and his ankle-bones received strength. And leaping up, he stood, and began to walk."

For two thousand years those who have had faith in Jesus and proclaimed their faith in His name have had proof that He is present as a dynamic life-giving force. Men and women with no previous healing power have suddenly become healers of marvelous ability. They do not claim to understand how the healing is done. They know only that through the exercise of faith and their word the spiritual quality in them is fused into unity with the power of Christ and the work is marvelously accomplished.

Cheerfulness Heals

→»»«←

The joy of health and happiness in Christ fills my body with new life, and I am made whole.

The love of the cheerful giver is expressed in me, and I feel Spirit pouring out its plenty into all my affairs.

→»»«←

E VERYBODY advocates cheerfulness as an aid to healing, but how few practice it as a vital part of the restorative principle? The large majority of sick persons are pessimists. They think they are much worse off than they are. They retard the healing efforts of nature and nature's God by repeated shocks of mental depression and fear of the serious character of some physical shadow as transient as "ships that pass in the night."

Some of our best doctors say that eighty per cent of humanity's ills would heal of themselves if left alone. In a book called "Let's Operate," by Dr. Roy H. McKay and Norman Beasley, we find this in italics:

104

"What people don't know, or won't believe, is that in eighty per cent of the cases they would get better without the ministrations of a physician, if they would merely go to bed and follow a proper diet."

To this the writers add:

"This applies to operations too. Every day a distressing number of unnecessary ones are being performed."

The authors of this book are not metaphysicians. Doctor McKay is an eminent surgeon. He says in his preface, "This book was written with great reluctance."

So we find that good doctors, who have the welfare of humanity at heart, are advising that we do not race to the operating table at the first sign of pain.

"Be of good cheer." The intelligence that created your body knows how to repair it. Get still, relax, turn your attention to the sustaining life forces within your organism. Say to yourself,

I will fear no evil; for thou art with me.

Don't eat unless you are hungry. Many of our ills are caused by a greedy appetite that, in being satiated, clogs the body with surplus fuel. Jesus told His disciples that a certain type of devil (error) could be eradicated only by fasting and prayer. Then rejoice and be glad when you begin to feel the healing peace of Spirit creeping over you.

As we find cheerfulness conducive to health we

also find it paving the way for prosperity. Paul wrote, "God loveth a cheerful giver." If the Lord loves a cheerful giver, it must follow that He takes a more intimate interest in the finances of a happy person than in those of one who handles his money in a stingy fashion.

Make it a practice to put love and good cheer into all your finances, and you will open up sources of income that have stagnated because you have not given their mind substance an opportunity to flow into your affairs.

You have doubtless met commercial Jonahs— sunk in the waters of their own negative statements. Avoid their pessimistic thoughts and words. Bless what you receive; bless what you send out. God's plenteous substance moves in and through our mind constantly like a light shining in the darkness, but we do not comprehend it.

Cultivate the bountiful, cheerful spirit in every thought and act. Then your finances will flow harmoniously, and you will never lack any good thing.

Love Harmonizes

-->>)(((---

Thine harmonizing love is mine, and I am restored to peace and health.

Divine love, like a magnet, charges my mind and prospers my affairs.

-->>)(((---

AMONG PEOPLE who observe and think there is no question about love's being the greatest harmonizing principle known to man. The question is how to get people to use love in adjusting their discords. Where for a lifetime there has been continuous agitation for lawmaking and force as panaceas for the discords of humanity, the simple and easy methods of love seem childish and silly. The minds of reformers have as a rule been charged and surcharged with pictures of the unjust conditions in the world and their righteous indignation has often been excited to the boiling point. Their uppermost thought is how to outlaw or crush the oppressors. They fairly explode with indignation when love or some of its attributes is proposed as a remedy. This brings up the matter of the component parts of love, what the elements are that

107

constitute that very quiet and apparently powerless thing called love.

Paul says (I Cor. 13) that love is patience, kindness, generosity, contentment, modesty, goodness and good temper, truth, burden-bearing capacity, faith in everything, a hope for the happy outcome of everything, and never a thought of failure. These are some of the working parts of love, but not all. The fact is that love is fundamental in every activity of life, not only in the spiritual and mental but in the mechanical and physical as well.

Scientists describe gravitation as the force with which bodies attract each other. This definition holds good in the mental, in the physical, and for all we know, in the spiritual realm. So what the physicist calls gravitation is one of the activities of love. Withdraw for one instant the steady pull of love from mother earth and we, her children, would be plunged into the depths of space and darkness. We should remember this when we are tempted to think that no one loves us. The spiritually developed soul gives thought and attention to these apparently invisible yet powerful forces, and by repeated mental contacts it unifies spirit, soul, and body in the one Mind, which sustains and unifies all things.

It is through this process of unfolding love that great souls are developed. Men are not created great but with the capacity to become great. Many factors enter into soul growth, some minor and some major, but a soul never attains supermind power without love. The reason why love is essential in a great soul is that love is the binding power, the factor so necessary to strengthening or fortifying the soul. Hate and antagonism are disintegrating, and they destroy the cohesion of the spiritual electrons and protons of which the soul is built.

There are metaphysicians who think that this earth is a temporary abiding place of the soul, a kind of kindergarten, where lessons are learned in a single lifetime that fit the soul at death to fly away to paradise or some beautiful place in the skies. This line of thought separates the soul from its source and builds a mental gulf between soul and body. The body is the precipitation of the soul or thinking part of man; if it has developed sensuality and separation, it must be redeemed by being unified with the soul, and this unification is accomplished through love. When like Jesus we have developed love for all things, even for our enemies, then the body and all its elements become plastic to thought and we have all power in heaven and in earth. The energy of light, through which creative Mind rules heaven and earth, is amenable to man when his mind of love synchronizes with creative Mind and he can say, "I and the Father are one." According to physicists, nature in all its forms is an electromagnetic "solution" in which the atoms spin like cannon balls about one another; that is, nothing is solid, as it seems to be, but everything floats in ethereal space, ready to fly about at the impulse of a directive mind of superenergy such as that of Jesus. With this understanding we can see that Jesus was stating facts of superscience when He said to His disciples, "If ye have faith as a grain of mustard seed, ye shall say unto this mountain, Remove hence to yonder place; and it shall remove; and nothing shall be impossible unto you."

In his "Essay on Man" Pope must have had something akin to this combination of gravitation and love in mind when he wrote,

"When the loose mountain trembles from on high,
  Shall gravitation cease, if you go by?"

In us who are followers of Jesus in the regeneration, which engrafts upon the natural man the spiritual genius that causes him to develop superman power, it begins its work by inspiring us to do little things in love. From this doing grows larger capacities until we attain the full stature of the Christ man.

According to Revelations, Jesus said, "He that overcometh, I will give to him to sit down with me in my throne."

We begin our overcoming by thought mastery. We begin to master thoughts of hate and force by first thinking and doing the little component acts that constitute love. Begin today to be a little more patient. Practice kindness. Be generous in thought and act. When you are tempted to lose your temper, say, *"I have a good temper."* Affirm your truthfulness under all circumstances. If your burdens seem greater than you can bear, remember what Jesus said: "Come unto me, all ye that labor and are heavy laden, and I will give you rest." Develop spiritual faith by believing in spiritual forces capable of accomplishing for you the seemingly impossible. Affirm a propitious outcome for everything you plan or do, and never admit failure in anything.

"He that overcometh, I will give to him to sit down with me in my throne, as I also overcame, and sat down with my Father in his throne. He that hath an ear, let him hear what the Spirit saith to the churches."

Casting Out Fear

->)>|<<-

All-infolding God love and protection free me from every thought of fear, and I am strong and well.

My mind is filled and satisfied with Thine all-infolding substance, and all things are added.

->)>|<<-

IT IS THE unanimous verdict of students of the mind that fear is a paralyzer of mental action; also that fear weakens both mind and body. This being so universally conceded, it certainly is not worth while to call attention to that enfeebling state of mind but rather, on the other hand, to show how to keep from falling into its shadows and also how to overcome its habits. The majority of people will resent the statement that fear is a habit, but close observation proves to anyone that his fears are governed by repeated thoughts, words, and experiences. All fears rest upon thoughts, and if the thought foundation can be broken up the fear will vanish.

The mind imagines mountains of fears where no

real cause for fear exists. We live in a world where fear is taught as essential to safety. To begin with, we are told from infancy to "fear" God; then to fear evil in all its forms. With our mind crammed with fear images working night and day, how can we expect anything but the multitude of disasters that follow?

"Perfect love casteth out fear." Jesus taught love of God as the first commandment and love of neighbor as the second; there was no need for any other commandments. These two round out the law. Then the one and only effective remedy for fear and its ills is love.

We have all been told again and again that we must love God and our fellow man in order to fulfill the law of our being. Doubtless most of us have done this and have had the experience of very pronounced demonstrations of peace and protection in our life, yet we do not have that consciousness of love which we feel we should have when we think of God. There must be a reason for this deficiency, and there is. We have thought of love to God in terms of something of immense size, something that we must encompass as a whole, when the fact is that love is a composite. It is made up of attributes, as is made clear by Paul in I Corinthians.

According to Paul, love is the name of a great variety of little commonplace activities of everyday life. Are you patient and kind? "Love suffereth long, *and* is kind." Envious? "Love envieth not." Egotistical and proud? "Love vaunteth not itself, is

not puffed up." Are you temperamental? Love "doth
not behave itself unseemly." Are you grasping and
selfish? Love "seeketh not its own." Do you give
way easily to your temper? Love "is not provoked."
Do you behold evil as real and agonize over the
evils of the world? Love "taketh not account of
evil." Do you rejoice when disaster overtakes evil
persons and exclaim, "They got just what was coming to them"? "Love . . . rejoiceth not in unright-
eousness, but rejoiceth with the truth." Do you pa-
tiently bear "the whips and scorns of time"? "Love
. . . beareth all things." Are you open-minded and
receptive to good, whatever its source? "Love . . .
believeth all things." Do you anticipate the future
with fear and forebodings? "Love . . . hopeth all
things." Do you endure with trust and confidence in
eternal justice

"The oppressor's wrong, the proud man's contumely,
  The pangs of despised love, the law's delay,
  The insolence of office and the spurns
  That patient merit of the unworthy takes"?
Love "endureth all things." Paul says: "If I speak
with the tongues of men and of angels, but have
not love, I am become sounding brass or a clanging
cymbal. And if I have *the gift of* prophecy, and
know all mysteries and all knowledge; and if I have
all faith, so as to remove mountains, but have not
love, I am nothing. . . . But now abideth faith,
hope, love, these three: and the greatest of these
is love."

Nowhere in all literature do we find as clear an

analysis of love as here in this 13th chapter of I Corinthians. Those who have taken it as a guide to character discipline—that is, seeking to fashion their daily thinking by the standards set forth—have attained results so pronounced that they have been convinced of its being a panacea for all who are suffering from the ravages of distorted, God-less love.

The one and only remedy for the crosscurrents of fear is the restoration of the peace and harmony of life by love and its combinations.

Spiritual Hearing

→»«←

**I give ear to Thee and now realize Thy life
in all my members, for Thou art my health
unfailing.**

**My mind is full of Thy substance, and my
prosperity is always manifest in abundance.**

→»«←

THE SCRIPTURES are rich in references to the
listening ear. "He that planted the ear, shall
he not hear?"

Jesus said, "What I tell you in the darkness,
speak ye in the light; and what ye hear in the ear,
proclaim upon the house-tops." "He that hath ears
to hear let him hear."

In many places the Bible indicates the ear referred to is not the physical organ but the listening
mind or spirit. "Having ears, hear ye not?"

Then the question arises, Do we have ears that
can hear "overtones" from which the mind can
obtain meanings superior to those of the senses?
In every walk of life are those who stoutly claim
that they hear voices and sounds, musical and otherwise, inwardly or apparently with another set of

ears. Sometimes these persons are geniuses and sometimes they are classed as queer.

Physiology describes a complicated physical ear, but the "ear" that conceives and really hears is the auditory center in the brain. It is here the mind grasps and analyzes the sound vibrations. Thus musical people may have the same physical ears as the unmusical, but their minds have listened for the fine variations of sound and have given the auditory area in the brain a composer's ego. The great Beethoven was a brilliant example. He was stone-deaf when he composed some of the most beautiful music of the world. But his "inner ear" must have been open to music that is not heard by everyone.

What is true in music is also true in every religion, art, and science. Little Samuel heard the voice of the Lord. Joan of Arc heard militant voices. Modern psychics and many who are deeply religious hear voices, or sounds that they translate into voices, in their cerebral cortex. It is the bent of the mind that determines the character of the voice. Job said in substance that there is a spirit or mind in man that gives the breath or vibrations of the Almighty understanding.

Practice giving ear or listening with your mind to the Lord. You will acquire the ability to make contact with the mind radiations of Christ and concentrate them in your mind and actually hear His voice. On the contrary, by a like concentration of thought you can attract the mind of persons both in and out of the body and thereby become a psychic and medium. Excessive meditation on things spiritual also often dulls the receptivity of the outer ear and it loses its alertness.

Shakespeare says, "Give every man thy ear, but few thy voice"; that is, learn to listen rather than talk. Jesus called His first disciple Simon Peter. Simon means "hearing" and Peter "a rock." Spiritual receptivity is the basis of a solid character. We all need a fuller realization of life in order to be healthy. This can be attained by concentrating our attention on the universal life radiations and incorporating them into our mind and body.

This world of matter has its origin in a radiant substance that our mind conceives and automatically translates into flesh and physical things. The process is so gradual that we do not realize it, but modern science is daily approaching an explanation that will eventually be universally accepted; then what we are teaching from the spiritual side will be confirmed by the physical.

Light of Life

⇥»≪⇤

By Thy light and life I am strengthened and healed.

"Every good gift and every perfect gift" cometh from above, from the Father of light, and I am in all ways prospered.

⇥»≪⇤

IBLE WRITERS use the word "light" to represent intelligence. When Jesus said, "I am the light of the world," He undoubtedly meant that He was the expresser of Truth in all of its aspects. In the 1st chapter of John light and Truth are synonymous.

"There was the true light, *even the light* which lighteth every man, coming into the world." This does not mean that He was the light of all those who come into the physical world, but of those who are born of Spirit into the world of reality. Those who live in physical consciousness regard the light as a radiation of the sun through which people discern the outline of things. But within this light that chases away the darkness is a principle hidden from the sense man. "And the light shineth in the

119

darkness; and the darkness apprehended it not."
Materiality is unillumined and has no power in
itself to overcome its ignorance. So all attempts of
intellect to lift man and the human family to higher
states of consciousness will prove futile. There must
be an influx of spiritual energy and inspiration from
the "Father of lights."

Yet it is interesting to note how the discoveries
of modern science are demonstrating phases of
truth without bringing forth a single principle that
will raise man spiritually. For example, light has
been probed to its physical source and properties
have been revealed of a world that was nonexistent
to the physical man. Yet with all the marvelous
knowledge acquired about light no quality has been
revealed that man can apply to his moral or health-
restoring needs. The argument that light is a prop-
erty of electricity that is being successfully applied
to heal human ills is not borne out by facts.

Yet the Scriptures treat light and intelligence as
one. In the very first chapter of the Bible we are
told that Mind became manifest as light. "And
God said, Let there be light: and there was light"
But the mind that judges according to appearance
never discerns the inner truth about light or anything else.

We must know the Truth about the omnipresence
of the one intelligence in the light; then we shall
be made free from our intellectual darkness. Science
agrees with James that "every good gift and every
perfect gift is from above, coming down from the

Father of lights." Science says light is a very orderly and exceedingly productive wave motion in the ether, but science does not tell us that light is God intelligence in action and that we can link our mind with the light and reap the benefit of its marvelous potentialities.

Some Christian metaphysicians are shy about using the scientists' approach to their problems, fearing that they themselves will fall into a materialistic trend of thought. However when we see scientists telling in physical terms of the properties of God-Mind, needing only to add the assumption of an intelligent moving power, we have found the co-operation of a very earnest and convincing lot of truth seekers.

So do not be afraid of the true physical scientist, but give his discoveries the light of mind. Then you will find that the substance and life will become more obedient to your word of command.

Remember that Moses received his great command from Jehovah when he turned aside to see why the bush that burned was not consumed. Jehovah spoke to him "out of the midst of the bush"; that is, God was in the fire that lighted an ordinary bush. Open your mind to the light of Spirit wherever you are. See with the eye of the mind that God is omnipresent Spirit, "over all, and through all, and in all."

Thought Substance

-»>«<-

The Spirit of truth floods me with the light of life, and I am made whole.

The Spirit of truth reveals abundant Spirit substance, which I affirm to be the source of my prosperity.

-»>«<-

AGAIN the Spirit of truth opens our mind to God's law of supply and support, to the existence of a universal etheric thought substance prepared for man's body sustenance by infinite Mind. We have thought that in answer to our prayers God in some mysterious manner brought about the marvelous demonstrations that we had. Now we see that there has been prepared from the beginning an interpenetrating substance that, like a tenuous bread of heaven, showers us with its abundance.

But we must not only ask but bring the Spirit into consciousness by affirming its abundance to be the source of our prosperity. Then prosperity will begin to be manifested right in the face of apparent lack. Remember the invitation of the Master "Hith-

122

erto have ye asked nothing in my name: ask, and ye shall receive, that your joy may be made full." When we greatly desire to be just and honest and in all ways to express only that which is true under the divine law, our soul radiates energy waves into the ether that produce the color blue. The aura around the bodies of sincere, honest persons is usually bright blue or some modification of blue. Blue is nearly always associated with white in representing spiritual ideals. The birth of Jesus was heralded by a bright star in the blue vault of heaven, and the stars in our American flag have a blue background.

Some persons think that when they quit lying they are demonstrating Truth. This is commendable, but falls short of fulfilling the complete reformation of the Spirit of truth. In the Gospel of John Jesus repeats in chapter after chapter the promise that He will send to those who believe on Him a Comforter, whom He calls "the Spirit of truth." In the 15th chapter we read, "But when the Comforter is come, whom I will send unto you from the Father, *even* the Spirit of truth, which proceedeth from the Father, he shall bear witness of me." In the 16th chapter we find these words: "I have yet many things to say unto you, but ye cannot bear them now. Howbeit when he, the Spirit of truth, is come, he shall guide you into all the truth." "And I will pray the Father, and he shall give you another Comforter, that he may be with you for ever, *even* the Spirit of truth . . . for he abideth with you, and shall be in you."

Never in the history of the world have there been so many religious cults as now. It is "Lo, here! or, There" the world round. To one who is not well grounded in the fundamental principles of Truth this is all very confusing. Jesus warned us to beware of man-made religions: "Go not . . . after *them*." "The kingdom of God cometh not with observation." "The kingdom of God is within you."

By exercise of his innate independence man lost his awareness of Spirit and was consequently cast out of the Garden of Eden or "paradise of God." Those of us who are getting an understanding of the divine law are becoming aware again of the Spirit that rules in this wonderful kingdom of the mind.

The Spirit of truth is the mind of God in its executive capacity; it carries out the divine plan of the originating Spirit. It proceeds from the Father and bears witness of the Son. We have in the operation of our own mind an illustration of how Divine Mind works. When an idea is fully formulated in our mind and we decide to carry it out, our thoughts change their character from contemplative to executive. We no longer plan, but proceed to execute what we have already planned. So God-Mind sends forth its Spirit to carry out in man the divine idea imaged in the Son.

It is very comforting to know that there is a Spirit co-operating with us in our efforts to manifest God's law. God in His divine perfection has seemed so far removed from our human frailties that we have lost heart. But now we see that Jesus taught that God is intimately associated with us in all our life's problems and that we need only ask in His name in order to have all fulfilled.

The Spirit of truth is God's thought projecting into our mind ideas that will build a spiritual consciousness like that of Jesus. The Spirit of truth watches every detail of our life, and when we ask and by affirmation proclaim its presence, it brings new life into our body and moves us to observe hygienic and dietary laws that restore health.

Intensified Zeal

→⟫⟪←

The zeal of God quickens, vivifies, and vitalizes both mind and body and makes me every whit whole.

My zeal for spiritual things increases, and I am abundantly prospered, praise God!

→⟫⟪←

PERSONS with poise and purpose, holding themselves well in hand, regard with some suspicion those who are unduly zealous. When zeal runs away with judgment, energy is wasted and confidence blasted. The fires of zeal are soon burned out and the cause of its champion may be slightingly referred to as "flashes in the pan." Nevertheless, zeal, intensity, enthusiasm, is essential to the achievement of any and every great purpose.

We usually judge zeal by the noise it makes. But noise is not characteristic of the zeal that overcomes seemingly insurmountable obstacles and wheels them into line with its quiet yet mighty energy of purpose. When you see men and women working steadily and unselfishly toward some cherished goal, do not conclude that they are moved by some selfish motive, the attainment of which will give them personal pleasure. They are fired by an impulse of soul that boils with an inward flame and urges them onward, regardless of the outer mind of caution and conservatism.

The trait of man named variously zeal, enthusiasm, intensity of soul, is a prime faculty of spiritual man. It is found in one of the disciples of the type man Jesus, and its character is revealed in his name, Simon the Zealot.

Zeal's throne or center of activity in the body is at the base of the brain, in the medulla. It is the seat of the animal soul, and its office is to vaporize the fine nerve fluid and distribute it to the senses. The medulla performs in the body the work of the carburetor in a motorcar.

An intense desire to carry out some idea forces the nerve fluid into the medulla, where it is atomized with inspiration (air) and then flared through the optic nerve to the eye, where the Spirit ignites it, and it flashes into light. "It is the Spirit that giveth life."

When the Spirit moves a man from within to the accomplishment of some cherished ideal and the intellect steps in and says it can't be done, a conflict ensues and the natural flow of the volatile body is impeded. Congestions and clots form in the circulation, the man gradually slows down, and what are called the marks of old age appear. This is why man should never give up the quest for greater and better expression of God-given abilities.

The hop, skip, and jump, the buoyancy and joy of youth, should be cultivated and continued more enthusiastically as the years advance. The idea that man grows feeble with years is a foolish fallacy. The longer one lives the better one should know how to live.

The attention of the followers of Jesus in the regeneration is called to the many lessons and warnings that He gave regarding man's zeal for commercialism. He rebuked Satan, the adverse mind, for suggesting that He demonstrate how to turn stones into bread. He warned, "Lay not up for yourselves treasures upon the earth." One of His earliest works was putting the commercial activities out of His body temple. "Take these things hence; make not my Father's house a house of merchandise."

Then His disciples remembered that it was written, "Zeal for thy house shall eat me up." Jesus explained that the "house" He referred to was His body. He was cleansing His body of a dominant race thought, the desire to accumulate money.

The people of the world today are so zealous for the solution of economic problems that they have forgotten God. They do not ask for wisdom to guide them in the nation's industrial affairs, but they plan and scheme and wrangle and get deeper and deeper in debt; that is, into the clutches of the beast of greed that puts its mark of slavery upon all who worship it.

Be zealous for spiritual realities. Lay up for yourselves treasures in the heavens.

The Unreality of Error

-»>«<-

My understanding of Truth reveals the unreality of sickness and the reality of health. I am radiant with the understanding that abiding health is my divine inheritance.

My understanding of the omnipresence of elemental substance opens the door to a continuous inflow of superabundance into my mind and affairs.

-»>«<-

LACK OF understanding, not only individual but collective, confronts us on every side. We blunder through life instead of walking confidently, open-eyed. Or we sit in the City of Indecision waiting for something to turn up when, urged and guided by the inner light, we should be going forth to meet good fortune.

We never weary of quoting that wise observation of Job's "There is a spirit in man, and the breath of the Almighty giveth them understanding." Most persons think that understanding is gained by intellectual development, mostly in institutions of learning. But the Book of Job was written by one who had great understanding but no literary degrees, so far as is known. Some authorities claim the book is at least five thousand years old; but Job knew much about Spirit both in Jehovah and in man. In the passage quoted he uses the pronoun "them" instead of "he" in referring to man, thus revealing that he understood the spiritual nature of man to be dual: male and female. Job's familiarity with Spirit and spiritual laws is evidence to a metaphysician that he gained his understanding direct from Spirit. Jesus taught, "It is the spirit that giveth life."

We would not belittle intellectual knowledge if it is acquired under the guidance of Spirit. The one and only object of man's existence is the development of his soul, and any attainment, whether mental or material, that cannot be associated with and counted as an aid toward that end will ultimately be refused. So it is the concentration of the mind upon Spirit that reveals the truth about the many situations that meet us in our daily contacts. If we count health and disease as equal, the "thought stuff" of our mind will animate them with like potency. We shall find ourselves believing that disease is just as real and far more catching than health.

Yet a moment's analysis of the relation between disease and health shows that health is the real, the God-given condition, and disease the unreal, the abnormal, from which we are all seeking to escape. Truth not only shows the reality at the core of all things; it also shows that we shall never escape from the unreal so long as we allow our mental processes to clothe it with "thought stuff."

If you deny disease as devoid of reality and affirm health as spiritual and abiding, the Spirit will bear witness with your spirit and you will demonstrate health.

Daily concentration of mind on Spirit and its attributes reveals to man that the elemental forces that make matter are here in the ether awaiting our recognition and appropriation. It is not necessary to know all the details of the scientific law in order to demonstrate prosperity. Go into the silence daily at a stated time and concentrate on the substance of Spirit prepared for you from the foundation of the world. You will thus open up a current of thought that will bring prosperity into your affairs.

Joy Radiates Health

->>><<<-

The joy of Jesus Christ sets me free, and I
am healed.

I rejoice as I realize Thine all-providing plan
now fulfilled in me.

->>><<<-

N OW WE HAVE reports of a sanitarium where
laughter is the only healing remedy. Time
was when such an institution would not
only have been subject to the ridicule of the com-
munity but its promoters would doubtless have come
under the insanity regulations. But now that not
only psychology but medical therapy is giving attention to the effect of the emotions on the health, the
systematic cultivation of joy is looked upon favor-
ably as a healing agent.

"A glad heart maketh a cheerful countenance;
But by sorrow of heart the spirit is broken."

Solomon or some other wise author of Proverbs
wrote that thousands of years ago, and it is good
doctrine today. The historical records of the race
go back about six thousand years, and it is found

that people have changed very little in their dominant characteristics during that time. Solomon, reputed the wisest man of his age, rendered his judgments from the testimony of the emotions rather than the facts as they were given in his court. The Bible tells of his appeal to the love of the two women who claimed the same infant as their child, calling for a sword to divide it so that each woman might receive half. The real mother begged that the sword should not be used, and of course the case was decided in her favor.

Legend says that Solomon amazed the Queen of Sheba by his quick solution of problems that she proposed. She dressed a group of boys and girls in exactly the same clothes and demanded that he tell the sex of each. He ordered basins of water for them to wash their hands in. The boys all plunged their hands in the water and got sodden cuffs, while the girls carefully rolled up their sleeves. Then a combination of real and artificial flowers were brought in; the queen demanded that Solomon point out the difference. He sent for a swarm of bees and readily made a decision. The queen was so pleased with Solomon's wisdom that she made him a love offering equal to three hundred and sixty thousand dollars.

In our modern practice of spiritual healing we find sadness and sorrow to be the cause of many physical ills. We also find that happiness is natural to man and that he can release it from his inner life through an understanding of Truth.

The study of the spiritual side of life awakens in mind, and even in body, emotions that convince one of the reality and eternal continuity of life, regardless of the changes that take place in outer manifestation.

Isaiah had a consciousness of this when he wrote in the 35th chapter of his book: "And the ransomed of Jehovah shall return, and come with singing unto Zion; and everlasting joy shall be upon their heads; they shall obtain gladness and joy, and sorrow and sighing shall flee away."

Zion represents spiritual peace, a peace that comes to those who attain an understanding and consciousness of Spirit and its activities in the soul.

Sorrow used to be considered a virtue among religious people, but this notion is being dissolved among the enlightened. Death has been the greatest source of sorrow, but evidence that the soul continues to live after it leaves the body is being produced from so many sources that the sense of separation is being rapidly removed, and many people now believe that we continue to exist as thinking entities whether in the body or out of the body.

Of all men who have lived on earth Jesus understood best the joy of the spiritual life, and He had the power of imparting that joy.

"He shall weep and lament, but the world shall rejoice: ye shall be sorrowful, but your sorrow shall be turned into joy." "These things have I spoken unto you that my joy may be in you, and *that* your joy may be made full."

"Selah!"

—»×«—

I have set the Lord always before my face,
therefore my heart is glad and my flesh
resteth in confidence.

I have faith in Thee as my unfailing resource,
and I am in all ways prospered.

—»×«—

"I HAVE SET Jehovah always before me:
Because he is at my right hand, I shall not
be moved.
Therefore my heart is glad, and my glory rejoiceth:
My flesh also shall dwell in safety."

The Psalms constituted the hymnbook of the
early church, and no finer example of religious
fervor and devotion and literary excellence can be
found in the lyrics of any people.

Although the author of the Psalms is usually referred to as David, that great poet and musician is
by critics credited with considerably less than half
of the one hundred and fifty hymns that appear in
the Bible.

Psalm means "lyric," and the heading of each indicates to the musician what attitude of devotion
should precede its rendition. "Selah" is the most

135

common heading. Bible authorities are not all agreed as to its precise meaning, but a very general opinion is that it means "pause," "silence," "to be still." But why pause before the music has even begun? Just here is where an understanding of spiritual law helps one. Before any act that involves direct appeal to God there should be a silent recognition of God's presence, of Jehovah-shammah, "The Lord is present," which is one of the sacred names of Jehovah.

In all our prayers, talks, and songs with God as the subject, we should first have a period of silence, a selah, in which the divine presence is invoked as the creative power. Then we can proclaim with Jesus, "I speak not from myself: but the Father abiding in me doeth his works." The heading of Psalm 16 is "Michtam of David." One authority says michtam means "gold," another "excellence," and still another "mystery." It means all of these and more. Beginning at verse 8, we have a prophecy of the supreme overcoming demonstrated by Jesus:

"I have set Jehovah always before me:
  Because he is at my right hand, I shall not be
    moved."

Jehovah is the name of the supermind in man and is called the Christ in the New Testament. Give first place in all your thoughts and acts to this all-powerful presence and you will realize the "right hand" of guidance and steadfast conviction.

A "glad" heart speeds up the circulation and

sweeps effete matter from the blood stream; then the flesh rests in confidence and health appears.

The prosperity word is one that we have often used in our Unity prayer ministry during the past fifty years. Some of you may cast it aside as threadbare, but don't be hasty. You may have used it many times, with varying degrees of success, but no one has exhausted its possibilities.

The producing power of a word depends on the ability of its user to uncover its inner meaning and apply it to his particular needs. When you use the word "Thee," do you think what its antecedent is? You will quickly say "God," but "God" covers a multitude of creative forces. In this case you are working to bring prosperity into your affairs; hence you should fill your mind with images and ideas of the all-providing, all-supplying One. Ancient Hebrew seers and adepts like Moses and Elijah understood this, and they had seven sacred names for Jehovah, each of which represented Him in His specific creative ability.

Jehovah-jireh means "Jehovah will provide," and anyone who concentrates his mind on this mighty One and persistently affirms His presence and power visible and invisible will be provided for regardless of any opposing circumstances. Should the Lord seem to be absent, use the hidden name of this mighty presence. Jehovah-shammah ("the Lord is present"), and you will soon feel the dynamic life and substance of creative Mind charging the ether with its living productiveness.

Spiritualizing the Intellect

→⟫⟪←

I separate myself in consciousness from the
mind of the flesh, that I may enter into the mind
that was in Christ Jesus.

→⟫⟪←

THIS affirmation is a good one to take into
the inner consciousness, and we would em-
phasize the word "consciousness." This whole
matter of soul unfoldment depends upon the consciousness that we have.

We have no independent mind—there is only
universal Mind—but we have consciousness in that
Mind, and we have control over that consciousness.
We have control over our own thoughts, and our
thoughts fill our consciousness. By analyzing ourselves we find that we unconsciously separate our
self into different personalities. Now we should do
this work consciously. We should enter into the
understanding that the I AM power (all power) is
given unto us in consciousness, and then join or
unify this consciousness with the great Christ Mind.

Thus the central idea in this word of affirmation
that we are seeking to understand and to incorporate
into our consciousness is the Christ Mind. As spiritual metaphysicians we find that the Christ Mind
is the Mind of Spirit. In the consciousness of man

it functions as two states of consciousness: one in the flesh, the other in the Spirit. But the mind of the Spirit is the source of all.

In daily worship it is well to impress upon the sensitive mind that it is unified with Divine Mind through Christ, through the same mind that was in Christ Jesus.

Understanding this as the basic principle of our thought and realizing the power of thought to impress itself upon the sensitive plate of man's mind, we find this prayer invaluable:

I separate myself in consciousness from the mind of the flesh, that I may enter into the mind that was in Christ Jesus.

First we disentangle our thoughts from the flesh and lift our consciousness up to Spirit. We hold them steady in spiritual consciousness until they begin to get hold of Spirit essence, Spirit power, Spirit love. Everything that we see in the manifest comes from this one Spirit-mind; so it is well to hold this affirmation until the most sacred ethers respond to our realization:

I separate myself in consciousness from the mind of the flesh, that I may enter into the mind that was in Christ Jesus.

When considering the value of prayer and realization we call to mind the case of Jacob and Esau receiving the blessing of their father Isaac.

It was customary to give the first-born the prior

blessing, and this blessing of the first-born belonged to Esau. But through the connivance of the mother, Rebekah, and Jacob himself, Jacob got the blessing, and of course by a subterfuge. The procedure was really a dishonest one, and Esau was wroth with his brother Jacob for taking his blessing and threatened his life. The mother advised Jacob to flee to the country of her brother Laban, and Jacob immediately set out on his journey. He was however in a wilderness of thought.

As metaphysical Christians we take this scripture to be a spiritual history of man as well as a history of outer events. We try to read it in the spirit appropriate to it. Spiritual things must be spiritually discerned. The Bible is a spiritual book. We arrive at a greater understanding and enhance our interest in the different characters of Jacob and Esau when we look upon them not only as individuals but as representatives of the race as a whole.

If we study the four characters of Isaac, Jacob, Esau, and Rebekah, we find that they represent dominant ideas in man, ideas that pertain to his very being, that are of vital interest. As we read out of the law we find that Esau—a hunter, a person subservient to his bodily appetites, a man of the flesh—represents the flesh, the body. A person of a little different turn of mind, a man who loved home and the quiet spiritual things of life, Jacob represents the mind, the intellectual man.

Of course in the process of evolution the natural man comes first. Then the spiritual man begins to unfold in us. Here in the Bible story we find that the spiritual man, or rather the intellectual man illumined by Spirit, gets the blessing. The Israelites set great store by this blessing. Rightly understood, a blessing is a great source of inspiration. It lays a firm foundation in the mind, and it brings out the good. A curse sees the evil and emphasizes it; but a blessing sees only the good and emphasizes only the good. Thus we come to see the importance for the soul's evolution of an understanding of the development of these two Biblical characters.

As we look at the blessing that Isaac gave Jacob and Esau—for he did bless Esau after he had blessed Jacob, though he gave Esau the blessing that would bring out his character—we discover that he was governed by law. The blessing he gave Jacob was one upon the mind and not upon the body; in fact, it was a blessing of the part of the race mind concerned with service, the part that has to do with the exercise of authority.

In this blessing there is a calling forth of those inherent faculties of the mind which enter into the exercise of authority. "Let people serve thee." The mind dominates the body. "Let . . . nations bow down to thee." We also see nations being dictated to by some mind, some dictator.

> "Let thy mother's sons bow down to thee:
> Cursed be every one that curseth thee,
> And blessed be every one that blesseth thee."

Here we can see the power of ideas to bless or to

curse. We see that he who uses his mind to curse gets the curse in return, while the mind that blesses receives blessings in return.

If we study our mind we find that it is radiating energy constantly and that whatever we send out comes back. This is true of the mind of man, and we see it in evidence everywhere, not only individually but collectively.

To Esau Isaac said,

"Behold, of the fatness of the earth shall be thy
    dwelling,
And of the dew of heaven from above;
And by thy sword shalt thou live, and thou shalt
    serve thy brother."

Here in these symbols we have the body man or man of the flesh. "The fatness of the earth shall be thy dwelling": man lives very close to the earth. "And by thy sword shalt thou live": the man of flesh is sent forth by the man of the mind to carry out his warring ideas. Intellectual man is the general or the governor or the dictator that sends the man of the flesh to do his biddings.

"And it shall come to pass, when thou shalt break
    loose,
That thou shalt shake his yoke from off thy neck."

In the evolution of man, the body (Esau) finally comes into its own. The Isaac blessing is carried out in the world today. We find that the working classes

that have been under the yoke of the intellect—
the intellectual man—now are beginning to assert
themselves. They are breaking loose from the yoke
of bondage to the intellect, the mind; the flesh is
beginning to assert itself. We are giving more attention to the flesh every day. People are awaking
to the fact that the body is an important part of
man, and so we see everywhere the fulfillment of
this blessing.

If we study ourselves, we find a tendency toward
the working out of the two minds. The tendency of
the intellect is to dominate, to have its way and
ignore the body. But the body is beginning to break
loose from this bondage and demand its own. It is
saying to us: "Why, I am a very important part of
this world. You can't leave me and go off to some
faraway place. I am an important part of you." So
with Esau the flesh begins to break loose from this
dominance of the mind that has separated it from
the good things of the heavenly estate. We raise it
up, and it begins to become a power in the world.
We must soon come to a place in our national,
social, and economic evolution where the earth and
all that it has will be recognized in a larger way,
become an integral part of our life. This is very
clearly taught in this story of the mind and the
heart. Isaac (the I AM) recognized this unity and
brought it into expression in his blessings of his two
sons.

We have these two "sons," the mind and the
body. It is the mind that connects us with Principle.

Jacob made this connection, but Esau had as yet
failed to come to the place where he could recognize that he was a son of God. Jacob took that
blessing from him. He became the sole representative
when he was really the secondary one, but he forged
ahead in the race; and so we have today the intellect dominating almost everything. It is evident
that the Jacob faculty (the illumined intellect) has
assumed its prerogative in the world today. The
illumined intellect rules. God is omnipresent, God
is intelligence, just as much in our mind as anywhere. The blessing of the I AM consciousness brings
out the intelligence that has the greatest ruling
power. But we find that we must also bless the body
as well as everything connected with it.

As we study the Bible we find that after he broke
away from the material consciousness Jacob had
many experiences. He went into another state of
consciousness (another country), in which he was
awakened spiritually to a still higher plane. In the
16th verse of the 28th chapter of Genesis we read:
"And Jacob awaked out of his sleep, and he said,
Surely Jehovah is in this place; and I knew it not."
He was in the sleeping state of consciousness. He
had a dream and saw a ladder extending from the
earth up into heaven and angels or messengers of
God ascending and descending it. Jehovah was at
the top of this ladder, and He told Jacob that he
was to be the father of a great nation and that a
certain blessing was to be poured out upon him.
When Jacob awoke he saw that God was in the

place where he was; that the place was the very "house of God," the dwelling place of God.

In other words, here was evidence of omnipresence. Each individual must have his first awakening to the truth that God is everywhere and that, whatever may be the place, God is there as omnipresent Spirit-mind. In this instance Jacob was surrounded by rocky hills, and he piled up stones and made an altar to Jehovah right there. The great lesson for us is that God is everywhere, no matter how material the surroundings may seem to be. To the unregenerate man there is usually a great awakening in an experience of this kind.

When man begins to see beneath the surface and to realize that God is with him constantly, he seeks to make a union with infinite Mind, omnipresent God-Mind. The Scripture reads: "And Jacob vowed a vow, saying, If God will be with me, and will keep me in this way that I go, and will give me bread to eat, and raiment to put on, so that I come again to my father's house in peace, and Jehovah will be my God, then this stone, which I have set up for a pillar, shall be God's house: and of all that thou shalt give me I will surely give the tenth unto thee."

Here was a covenant or an agreement made by a man at the moment of his first great illumination as regards the one omnipresent substance. He may have realized before that God was the great I AM, the Jehovah, leading him, but he did not realize that this earthly substance, the rocks about him, were really representative: that they are a part, a living part, of the God substance; that the I AM man in his illumination has a share in that substance; that it is his substance through infinite Mind. The covenant of Jacob to give one tenth of all his increase was the real beginning of what in modern times we call tithing: making God a partner in all our finances.

Jacob became a great financier of the ancient world, and through the illumination that he got from Jehovah he knew how to take advantage of every opportunity.

We do not take Jacob as an example of how man should handle his finances, for he was something of a trickster. In truth he represents the trickery and cunning of the world in this field. But apparently Jehovah, the one Mind, was with him. Sometimes there are contradictions that we cannot always understand; but when we know that we are the directive power as regards all that belongs to us, we may get on financially. But in the end there is an adjustment, illustrated in the meeting of Jacob and Esau at the ford Jabbok.

But with it all Jacob loved Jehovah and shared his wealth with the Lord. He proved the law of tithing, that tithing is one of the foundation principles of financial success. Man can become a great possessor of the substance of this world if he follows certain rules of tithing. Jacob gives us the key, which is the recognition that God is all substance, and that if man wants to handle this substance wisely and well, if he wants to handle it for great material success, he should do what Jacob did: take God into partnership with him.

There is an omnipresent economic Mind, and if a man begins to deal with this economic Mind he will have a partner that has all resources.

If you want to become a rich man, if you want to be possessed of every good thing in the world, take God as your partner, incorporate His mind into your mind, in your daily giving. Give of your substance with the thought that it is God's money you are handling. Realize that it is His tenth that you are giving for His glory. With this thought in your mind you will begin to attract new spiritual resources, and things will begin to open up in your affairs. You will know that infinite Mind is with you. That is what Jacob realized, and he attained great success in his affairs. I would say to everyone who wishes to demonstrate prosperity: take God into partnership with you and you will demonstrate abundance.

The Sevenfold Cleansing

→»«←

*Go and wash in the Jordan seven times, and
thy flesh shall come again to thee, and thou
shalt be clean.*

THE 5th chapter of II Kings relates the healing
of Naaman by Elisha. Naaman was the cap-
tain of the hosts of Syria, but he was a leper.
The Syrians had brought away captive out of the
land of Israel a little maiden, who waited on Naaman's wife. She said to her mistress, "Would that
my lord were with the prophet that is in Samaria!
then would he recover him of his leprosy."

The incident was told to the King of Syria and
he sent a letter, with presents of silver, gold, and
raiment, to the king of Israel, requesting that he
heal his general, Naaman. When the King of Israel
read the letter he rent his clothes and said, "Am I
God, to kill and to make alive, that this man doth
send unto me to recover a man of his leprosy? but
consider, I pray you, and see how he seeketh a
quarrel against me."

When Elisha heard of it he sent word, "Let him
come now to me, and he shall know that there is
a prophet in Israel."

So Naaman came with his horses and with his
chariots and stood at the door of the house of

Elisha. And Elisha sent a messenger to him, saying, "Go and wash in the Jordan seven times, and thy flesh shall come again to thee, and thou shalt be clean."

But Naaman was wroth and went away and said, "Behold, I thought, He will surely come out to me, and stand, and call on the name of Jehovah his God, and wave his hand over the place, and recover the leper. Are not Abanah and Pharpar, the rivers of Damascus, better than all the waters of Israel? may I not wash in them, and be clean?" So he turned and went away in a rage.

And his servants came near and spoke to him and said, "My father, if the prophet had bid thee do some great thing, wouldest thou not have done it? how much rather then, when he saith to thee, Wash, and be clean?"

Then he went down and dipped himself seven times in the Jordan, according to the saying of the man of God; and his flesh came again like the flesh of a little child, and he was clean.

This demonstration of spiritual healing doubtless took place just as related, and again and again it has been a source of encouragement to those who have believed in the healing power of God. But to all who read scripture in the spirit this narrative is rich in clues to a method of healing for all men who can discern and use the law set in action by Elisha.

Elisha is often referred to by the Bible commentators as a forerunner of Jesus. His marvelous works are easily recognized as proceeding from the same Spirit that inspired Jesus, and his gentleness and simplicity are paralleled only by those of the great Master.

It is not difficult to see in Elisha an incarnation of the Christ, and he was in a certain degree Christ manifest. Jesus was a fuller manifestation of the same Christ.

If we admit that Elisha is a type of Christ—that is, of the Jehovah or supreme I AM of man—we should admit with equal readiness that the other characters in the narrative are types of various powers or traits common to all men.

Starting with a certain understanding of man in the three departments of his being, spirit, soul, and body, we discern Naaman to represent the will, Syria the intellect, the king of Israel the ruling power in the domain of intellectual thought. The "little maiden" is representative of a rudimentary intuition that has been captured by the intellect and is being made to serve its ends. The river Jordan is the life current flowing into man's subconscious nature from the one great life. This "river of life" is the source of the natural healing impulse that constantly reconstructs and restores the organism.

The will through its conquests in the sense world has gained the applause of men and is called "great," "honorable," "mighty." This exaltation of will stimulates the personal ego until it ignores any power higher than itself. This supreme egotism stops the flow of spiritual life in the organism and body atrophy sets in. Pride and ambition cut the invisible channels that connect soul and body with the great river of life. The blood then loses its elixir and the flesh its glow of health; decay of skin and extremities follows and the man becomes a leper.

The only remedy for the starved body is the relinquishment by the will of its haughty assumption of dominion. No new life can flow in until the will unclamps its affirmations of supremacy. All men and women belong to the Naaman family, and no one is wholly exempt from the limitations of personal will until he has said with Jesus Christ meekness, "Not my will, but thine, be done."

Intuition (the little feminine Israelite) points the way to the representative of Jehovah who dwells in Samaria. Personal will loves to make display of worldly possessions and goes to the simple, unpretentious Elisha with a great retinue of servants, horses, chariots, besides presents of silver, gold, and rich raiment. He expects the prophet to call upon his God, wave his hands over the place, and make a great display in the healing. But the gentle prophet tells him in his simple way to bathe in the Jordan seven times. Naaman is wroth at being told to do so slight a thing when he had come so far as such a great outlay. He had expected the prophet to recognize his exalted position and give him special attention. To do such a puerile thing as to bathe in an insignificant stream like the Jordan filled him with indignation.

Teachers of Truth are constantly having to meet this egotism of the personal will in their students. The intellectual method of gaining knowledge is so ponderous: so many books have to be studied and so many things memorized that the simple methods of Truth are considered childish. In modern medical practice a paralytic might be dosed, serumed, X-rayed, and what not. Jesus healed such a case by simply saying, "Son, be of good cheer; thy sins are forgiven."

Jesus said He accomplished this through the faith of those who brought the sick to Him. There must be faith action before the forces that restore the life to the organism can be set in operation. The laborious methods of the medical profession are all for the purpose of stimulating the healing forces of nature. Nature is the servant of mind, and when lawful thoughts are enthroned in consciousness, nature restores the natural harmony existing between spirit, soul, and body. When the use of right thoughts and words is understood, nature's work is so easily accomplished that the intellectual man is nonplused and shakes his head with incredulity; or he goes away like Naaman, wroth at the seemingly crude and unheard-of prescription. However Naaman's servants prevailed upon him to give Elisha's remedy a trial, and when he had bathed in the Jordan seven times, "his flesh came again like unto the flesh of a little child, and he was clean."

The first step in all spiritual healing is faith, and the next is receptivity. Where the pride and fullness of intellect is dominant there is little opportunity for the subconscious stream of life to do its cleansing work. The proud Naaman must first be humbled before he can be healed, and the proud flesh be taken out of his heart before the proud flesh can be cured in his body.

Elisha apparently took no part in the healing, simply directing Naaman to bathe in the Jordan seven times. But there was a deep undercurrent of Spirit power at work in Elisha. He represented the higher self of the Naaman consciousness, which had been quickened. Jesus referred to this incident in Luke 4:27: "There were many lepers in Israel in the time of Elisha the prophet; and none of them was cleansed, but only Naaman the Syrian."

Elisha told Naaman to bathe in the Jordan seven times. Seven is a cardinal numeral and in ancient times was regarded as having mystical significance, that is, as symbolizing perfection, besides being loosely used for any indefinite considerable number, much as twenty or a hundred is used now. Peter used it in this sense when he said, "How oft shall my brother sin against me, and I forgive him? until seven times?" Jesus replied, "Until seventy times seven."

Seven is so universally used as a mystical number that there must be some reason for this in the fundamental arrangement of the natural world. In Solomon's Temple was the seven-branched candlestick. We know that this Temple represented the body of man and that the seven lights were symbols of seven centers in the organism, through which in-

telligence is expressed. Everybody knows five of
these centers: seeing, hearing, tasting, smelling,
touch. There are two in addition to these, which
we may call intuition and telepathy. The solar
plexus is the organism of intuition and the brain the
organ of telepathy.

All these centers of light have been dimmed
by sin. Hence sin has also been given a sevenfold
classification, *viz.,* pride, anger, lust, covetousness,
envy, gluttony, sloth. The great purifying river of
life must wash away these sins and their leprosy in
the body. To bring this to pass man must deny in
sevenfold measure the darkness of error that ob-
scures the inner light and life. These seven wash-
ings are to be repeated until the whole body is
clean.

The eye represents the discerning capacity of the
mind.

*My eyes are no longer darkened by thoughts of
deception, concealment, or lust. The cleansing
life and light of Spirit makes pure and clean
these eyes, and through all-seeing Mind I have
spiritual vision.*

The ear represents the receptive capacity of the
mind.

*My ears are no longer stopped by the sensitive-
ness and willfullness of the little self. I am no
longer bound by personality. I now bathe in
the great ocean of life, and I am free in bound-*

*less Spirit. I hear the voice of Truth only and
rejoice.*

The nose represents the initiative capacity of the
mind.

*The cleansing life of Spirit frees my mind of all
thoughts of fear, timidity, and incapacity. I am
bold, free, courageous Spirit, and I can do all
things through Christ.*

The tongue represents the judging capacity of
the mind.

*Sense appetite no longer clogs the clear discern-
ment of my spiritual judgment. The cleansing
life of Spirit quickens and cleanses my taste, and
I eat and drink only what my body requires
under divine law.*

Feeling represents the loving capacity of the
mind.

*I am no longer in bondage to the thought that
sensation is in matter. The cleansing life of
Spirit dissolves all fleshly lust for sense pleasure.
I am Spirit, and I desire the clean, pure currents of life to flow through every part of my
body, so that all may be made clean.*

Intuition is the natural knowing capacity of the
mind.

*The cleansing life of Spirit purifies my heart,
and I trust the "still small voice" within my soul.*

Telepathy is thought interchange.

The cleansing life of Spirit clears my mind of ignorance and materiality, and I see the activity of ideas and understand their import independently of human language. As God gave Daniel "knowledge and skill in all learning and wisdom: and . . . understanding in all visions and dreams," so He gives me and all His children the original ideas of His great mind to use as we will.

Prayer and Faith

→)(←

PRAYER is a science susceptible of being reduced to rules that prove it to be based upon demonstrable laws. The intellectual school of scientists will not accept our claim of science for prayer, because we operate in a field that they have not investigated. However "there are more things in heaven and earth . . . than are dreamt of" in their philosophy.

We who are testing out the laws of prayer cannot say with assurance that we have discovered and applied all of them so clearly that we can teach them to the multitude. The laws of prayer require a spiritually developed mind to give them full expression; hence not all persons are at once competent to cover the whole range of mental and spiritual activity requisite to the unfailing demonstration of prayer. Jesus taught that whatever we ask in prayer, believing, we shall receive.

So right at the beginning of our inquiry into scientific prayer we find a very vital condition emphasized and demonstrated by Jesus in His most effective prayers, and that is faith. We must have faith, though it be merely of mustard-seed size, before we can approach the fulfillment of the law of prayer.

Faith is the most mysterious of the spiritual fac-

158 Teach Us to Pray

ulties and has so far eluded the descriptive powers
of man. Many attempts have been made to describe
faith but with indifferent success. All spiritual metaphysicians agree that faith is an apprehension by
man of a mind power that connects matter and
spirit. Faith handles ideas with a facility similar to
that with which we handle pumpkin seeds. We plant
the little seeds in good soil and watch them grow in
a few months into large pumpkins. This is as great
a miracle as any that Jesus performed, the difference being that it takes time and an adjustment
of material instead of spiritual conditions.

But the scientific operation of the law of manifestation is just as mysterious in the one case as in
the other. However we find that we can improve
the conditions conducive to growth in the natural
world, and it is good logic to assume that we can
improve on the ancient practices of prayer. Primitive man had a sense of separation from his God.
He believed that through storm, lightning, thunder,
and earthquake his God was taking vengeance on
him for his misdeeds, and he prayed to be saved.
Then the most common form of prayer was the
prayer for favors and for vengeance on one's enemies. This form of prayer was popular among the
Israelites, as evidenced by their literature:

"Deliver me, O Jehovah, from mine enemies."

"Hide me under the shadow of thy wings,
From the wicked that oppress me,
My deadly enemies, that compass me about."

Although we have progressed somewhat in our attitude toward God the great majority of Christians are still begging a faraway God for favors.

What we all need is a better understanding of the principles at the very foundation of Being, of the spiritual character of God, and especially of the omnipresence of the spiritual principles. Then we need to understand our relation to these spiritual principles and what we have to do to make them operative in our mind and affairs.

We must know first that prayer is cumulative; that the more we pray the more we accumulate of the powerful spiritual energy which transforms invisible ideas into visible things. Paul said, "Pray without ceasing." Do not supplicate and beg God to give you what you need, but realize, affirm, and absolutely know that your supreme mind is functioning right now in God-Mind itself and that your thought substance and the spiritual substance of the Most High are amalgamated and blended into one perfect whole that is now being made manifest in the very thing you are asking for.

This is the modern technique of prayer, and it is being demonstrated by quite a few devout souls in this modern mechanical world. It is not emotional, nor do its devotees expect miracles; on the contrary, they apply the law of righteous thinking to a problem that has always been treated as outside the realm of exact science.

Every science under the sun has progressed and developed out of its early state of crudeness except

the science of the true character of God and of our
relation to Him. Now the time has come for us
to improve our methods of worship and reduce
them to scientific mind laws. When we fully realize
that God is a great mind in which "we live, and
move, and have our being," we shall begin to use
our minds in consonance with the Mind omnipresent.
Then a supreme harmony will be ours, and prayer
will become a divine soliloquy. As the entrancing
music of the modern world has been developed from
the primitive shepherd's playing his flute to his mate
and then falling in love with his own music, so we
shall unfold innate abilities of communion with
God and finally discover the divine harmony.

With this understanding then of the true character of prayer, let us give ourselves to prayer.

In its spiritual character our mind blends with
Divine Mind as the mist blends with the cloud.
Both are composed of the same elements and they
unite without friction if left to their natural affinity.
But give "the mist" the power and ability of separation and we have conditions that involve divisions
beyond enumeration. Man came out of God, is of
the same mind elements, and exists within the mind
of God always. Yet by thinking that he is separate
from omnipresent Spirit he has set up a mental state
of apartness from his source and he dwells in ignorance of that which is nearer to him than hands
and feet. A few moments of thought daily directed
toward God in acknowledgment of His presence
will convince anyone that there is an intelligence

always with us that responds to our thought when we direct our attention to it. Sometimes we automatically make this high contact when our mind is exalted by transcendent sights or sounds. The eminent astronomer Kepler had this experience when, viewing the expanse and majesty of the universe of stars, he inspirationally exclaimed, "O God, I am thinking Thy thoughts after Thee."

Much is heard about giving ourselves to service to the world, but how important is the self that we are offering? If we have found our real self the offer will be worth while, but if we are offering personality alone we shall never set the world afire.

Paul was a great example of an indefatigable minister. We can hardly conceive the hardships he endured. He enumerates a few of them in II Corinthians 11:24-28: "Of the Jews five times received I forty *stripes* save one. Thrice was I beaten with rods, once I was stoned, thrice I suffered shipwreck, a night and a day have I been in the deep; *in* journeyings often, *in* perils of rivers, *in* perils of robbers, *in* perils from *my* countrymen, *in* perils from the Gentiles, *in* perils in the city, *in* perils in the wilderness, *in* perils in the sea, *in* perils among false brethren, *in* labor and travail, in watchings often, in hunger and thirst, in fastings often, in cold and nakedness. Besides those things that are without, there is that which presseth upon me daily, anxiety for all the churches."

Paul was a tentmaker. He went from house to house preaching the gospel. At Troas Paul preached in a third-story room for several hours. About midnight a young man named Eutychus was overcome by sleep and fell from a window to the ground and was taken up dead. Paul went down and resurrected him, then went back to his preaching and kept it up until daybreak. A sermon twelve hours long would appall some ministers and all congregations, but not Paul.

"It matters not how strait the gate,
    How charged with punishment the scroll,
I am the master of my fate:
    I am the captain of my soul."

To Timothy Paul recommends, "Exercise thyself unto godliness." The word "exercise" is derived from a Greek word having the root meaning of "gymnastics." That is, train your mind to think about God as a force that can be incorporated into your mind as you incorporate strength into your body. If your mind is weak and flabby, practice thinking about God as strong and stable. This will lift your mind out of its depression and connect you with a never-failing source of stability and confidence. Thus in order of their importance and necessity take all the attributes of God, such as life, love, power, wisdom, and incorporate them into the muscles of your mind by exercise.

We are very apt to forget that the mind of man develops like his muscles, by exercise. The minister who thinks his education is complete when he leaves the theological seminary never becomes a great teacher of men. So the Christian who thinks he is saved when he has been "converted" will find that his salvation has just begun. Conversion and "change of heart" are real experiences, as anyone who has passed through them will testify, but they are merely introductory to the new life in Christ. When a person arrives at a certain exalted consciousness through the exercise of his mind in thinking about God and His laws, he is lifted above the thoughts of the world into a heavenly realm. This is the beginning of his entry into the kingdom of the heavens, which was the text of many of Jesus' discourses. When a man attains this high place in consciousness he is baptized by the Spirit; that is, his mind and even his body are suffused with spiritual essences, and he begins the process of becoming a new creature in Christ Jesus. Skeptics and the inexperienced view the changes in one's life produced by conversion as merely an emotional upheaval that will eventually pass away and leave the subject as he was before. No one is ever left exactly as he was before the experience. An effect has been produced on the soul structure that will never be wholly obliterated, but it may remain merely a temporary impression unless it is developed by exercise. This development cannot be accomplished by bodily exercise either. As Paul wisely says, "bodily exercise is profitable for a little; but godliness is profitable for all things."

The Healing Word

→»«←

EALING by the power of the word did not originate with Jesus of Nazareth, although it is from Him that we get our modern inspiration. In every age where man has realized the perfection of the original essence of Being and has spoken forth that realization, the result has been a restoration of things to their inherent harmony and order.

Whoever realizes that God is the underlying creative perfection and that man is His mouthpiece has laid the foundation for performing miracles of healing through the power of the word. But in order to do the miracles he must speak the word that he knows to be true.

Thousands in every age have caught sight of the truth of God's perfect being, but they have not been sure enough of their ground to go forth and proclaim it to a waiting world. Jesus of Nazareth was counted the Saviour of mankind because He freely proclaimed the truth about God and man. He not only proclaimed it, but He had faith in the power of His word to redeem men from the mental lethargy into which they had fallen.

"And Jesus went about in all Galilee, teaching in their synagogues, and preaching the gospel of the kingdom, and healing all manner of disease and all

164

manner of sickness among the people." The method of Jesus' healing has always been a theme that many have learnedly discussed and written about. The theories have been numerous, but they have nearly always been theories. The claim that He was the only Son of God, begotten in a certain manner to do a miraculous work, is also a theory to him who has not a clear understanding of what constitutes a son of God; hence it would be futile to discuss the things of Spirit with one who has not been quickened by Spirit.

Whatever these various theories of Jesus' remarkable healing power may be, none disputes one point: He used words as the vehicle of the healing potency. He always spoke to the patient "as *one* having authority." He had a certain assurance, an inner conviction, that He was speaking the truth when He said, "Thou art made whole"; and the result of His understanding carried conviction to the mind of the patient and opened the way for the "virtue" that went forth from the speaker. Notwithstanding this very apparent use of words by Jesus there has been a failure on the part of His followers to grasp their vitally important office in demonstrations. There has always been a belief in the religious world that there was somewhere a lost word that when found and spoken would set all things right. The Jews say this lost word is veiled in the name "Yahveh" and that its correct pronunciation is no longer known to men. They claim it was once known to their priesthood, and when it was used all the powers of God were manifest and mighty works were accomplished by it in brief moments of time.

All are familiar with the "God said" of Genesis in connection with the creation of the heavens and the earth.

Here at the very beginning the word is the creative agent, and John, personifying it, corroborates this. He says that in the beginning "the Word was with God" that it was God, and that all things were made by it, and without it was not anything made that has been made. The term that John used and that is translated "Word" in the King James New Testament has a much deeper significance than is usually given to it by Bible readers. It has been assumed by the church that "the Word" meant the personal Jesus Christ, and it has been so accepted.

The most thorough Greek scholars and all careful and honest Scripture authorities tell us that the Greek term *logos* has no equivalent in the English language; that it is untranslatable and should have stood in its original form instead of the accepted translation, "the Word."

Even in Greek the term *logos* has an inner meaning that only those of spiritual discernment can comprehend. Externally it covers both the spoken word and the underlying reason or valid premise; both being so intimately connected as to be one. This John conveys in saying that "the Word was with God, and the Word was God." Here is implied a distinction in office but a unity in purpose. With the early Fathers of the Greek Church the divine Logos had a peculiar significance which only those who had delved into the innermost of existence could comprehend.

Philo made the divine Logos the embodiment of all divine powers and ideas. He distinguished between the Logos inherent in God, corresponding to reason in man, and the Logos emanating from God, corresponding to the spoken word that reveals the thought. The former contains the ideal world; the latter is the first-begotten Son of God, the image of God, the Creator, the preserver, the giver of life and light, the mediator between God and the world. It is claimed that Philo wavered between a personal and an impersonal conception of the Logos, but leaned more to the impersonal.

Philip Schaff, speaking of the Logos, says:

"Saint John uses Logos (translated Word) four times as a designation of the divine, pre-existent person of Christ, through whom the world was made, and who became incarnate for our salvation (John 1:1-14; I John 1:1; 5:7, A.V.; Rev. 19:13). Philo may possibly have suggested the use of the term (although there is no evidence that John read a single line of Philo); but the idea was derived from the teaching of Christ, and from the Old Testament, which makes a distinction between the hidden and the revealed Being of God. There is an inherent propriety in this usage in the Greek language, where Logos is masculine and has the

double meaning of thought and speech. Christ as
to His divine nature bears the same relation to
God as the word bears to the idea. The word gives
shape and form to the idea, and reveals it to the
without. The word is thought expressed; thought is
the inward word. We cannot speak without the
faculty of reason, nor think without words, whether
uttered or not. The Christ-Logos is the Revealer and
Interpreter of the Hidden Being of God, the utter-
ance, the reflection, the visible image of God, and
the organ of all His manifestations to the world
(John 1:18; Comp. Matt. 11:27). The Logos was
one in nature or essence with God, yet personally
distinct from Him, and in closest communion with
Him."

In plain, everyday language, we would say that
Being, the original fount, is an impersonal principle;
but in its work of creation it puts forth the idea that
contains all ideas: the Logos, the Christ, the Son
of God, spiritual man. This idea is the creative
power, the concrete consciousness formulated by
universal Principle.

It is written of God: "Thou . . . art of purer
eyes than to behold evil." "Are not two sparrows
sold for a penny? and not one of them shall fall
on the ground without your Father." These pas-
sages seem paradoxical. When we understand that
in the first passage Principle is referred to, and in
the second the Logos or creative Father of Jesus,
then all is clear. Jesus always called the divine Logos
"Father." He never referred to it as an abstraction

but always as a being having intense love and compassion for all creation.

So He will become to each one who makes the conscious connection with Him. We shall realize that Being is not only principle so far as its inherent and undeviating laws are concerned, but also person so far as its relation to each one of us is concerned; that we as individuals do actually become the focus of universal Spirit, of the all-pervading and all-wise Logos, and that through us the universe is formed.

"And then shall they see the Son of man coming in clouds with great power and glory." Each one of us is a son of man, and our glory and power is in the keeping of the divine Logos.

We come into this power and glorify God just to the extent that we recognize and use the Logos. Jesus of Nazareth recognized and used it in its fullest sense. To Him it was not only an all-pervading principle of goodness and power but it was very much more; it was a near and dear Father, a Father whose interest in His children is greater than that of any earthly parent.

"If ye then, being evil, know how to give good gifts unto your children, how much more shall your Father who is in heaven give good things to them that ask him?"

We may make little out of the Logos and live in the shadow of its glory, or we may make much out of it and live in the sunshine of that glory. Some ask sparingly and receive in like measure; others ask largely and receive largely.

The Logos is the preserver and transmitter of the original spiritual ideas and essences of God. It is the sustainer upon which the universe rests, and all its creations are spiritually sequential, that is, logical. We are dependent upon it for every breath we draw. Its substance and intelligence are at the beck and call of prince and peasant alike, and in this sense it becomes the servant of all. All mold it into consciousness in the one and only way—through thought. Whatever you think about life or substance, that it becomes to you.

If you think the Logos will heal the sick through the power of your magnetic hand, you will do your healing in that way. If you think it will heal through your silent or spoken word, it will act accordingly. It will work for the ignorant and the wise, the wicked and the good, the poor and the rich. It is yours to use in whatsoever way you will. However the permanent results you get will be proportioned to your understanding of its whole nature. To grow in its grace and be glorified in the ineffable glory of the everlasting God you must know who it is you are dealing with.

Herein many are falling short in our day. They have been taught the manipulation of the Logos in its healing aspect and they are using it as a new therapeutic agent. To them it is a cold abstraction, a principle having intelligence and substance without consciousness. These qualities they handle as does the potter his clay. Instead of striving to attain that loving relation to the Father which should exist between parent and child, they are virtually introducing into their business world a new factor for the attainment of selfish ends. Do not let the icy hand of such a science grasp yours. Refuse to see the Father as anything less than the all-compassionate One who is interested in every act of your life, every thought you think; who has numbered even the hairs of your head. This is our God, the Most High Good, which dwells in our heart and soul and flames up into our mind with all the power of cleansing, healing, and uplifting. To this dear Father nothing is small, nothing is great. He does not ignore His creation; He does not stand afar off and view with the cold, critical eye of a connoisseur. His heart throbs with compassion; He sheds upon us the holy peace of His presence in the turmoil of sense, and we joyously exclaim, "Though all else fail me, in Thee I find rest."

Yet we must attain the full stature of the Godman. We must ultimately understand that the Father cannot be circumscribed by any human idea of Him or of what He should do for us. We must know that there is only good and that the word of good is the only permanently healing word. So long as we believe that the Father might heal at one time and not at another, that He might be induced to give us His healing Spirit under certain circumstances and not under others, we are misjudging His nature. If there is ever any limit to the healing power of the word, it is of our own manufacture.

The healing word is not a special creation to meet

an emergency. It is not a patent medicine prepared to cure specific diseases. The idea that it is a healing word at all originates in our limited notion that there is something that needs healing.

God is the supreme perfection; the Word is like unto that perfection. All its creations are perfect. It takes cognizance of the perfect only. When we realize this perfection and speak the words of Truth from that plane of understanding, the Word goes forth and establishes that which is. It does not heal anything—in its perfection there is nothing to heal. Its office is to behold the perfection of its Being; and as we do the works of the Father, we behold and restore that which is and always was perfect.

Thus he who realizes most thoroughly that God is the supreme perfection and that in Him can be no imperfection, and speaks forth that realization with conviction, will cause all things to arrange themselves in divine order.

This is being daily and hourly demonstrated by the faithful all over the land, thus proving true the nature of the Logos or Word of God. The meaning of the word *logos* is speech based upon reason. If the reasonable premise that God is the omnipresent God is well grounded in you, you cannot speak anything but healing and uplifting words. Your words must be for the healing of the nations, because they are true words flowing forth from a source in which Truth has no opposite.

If you believe that both good and evil conditions can be brought forth from this divine Logos, that both sweet and bitter waters can flow forth from the same spring, then your healing will be mixed. The spring is pure, and by letting your mind be an open way for its outpouring, you permit it to remain in its original purity and to cleanse all in whom you quicken it. If however you stop the flow here and there by an idea of limitation, by an idea of imperfection in the fount or in him upon whom the fount is being poured, you cut off its free currents to that extent.

Do not construe this to mean that you can pollute the stream by your thinking. This cannot be done; you simply refuse to let its purity come forth in its fullness. Like the lens that refracts the sunlight, you receive some rays that you do not throw upon the screen. The white light of Spirit is poured upon you, and your idea of limitation, in a given direction makes you opaque to some of its colors.

You are nothing less than a child of God and to you is intrusted the creative power. When you realize this you can go forth forgiving men their sins as you have forgiven your own.

The word of God is spoken through the Son of man. You are a son of man, and it is your duty to be about your Father's business, healing the sick, casting out demons, forgiving the sinful, and spreading the gospel of a living God.

But the "word is very nigh unto thee, in thy mouth." Speak it forth and demonstrate, as did Jesus, that "the Son of man hath authority on earth to forgive sins." What is sin? Is it anything other than an erroneous way of attaining happiness? God is happy, and it is a state natural to us all or we would not strive for it. There must also be a way to reach it. If we have not reached it by the way we have followed, we have but to turn about and seek another way. Repenting is turning about, letting go of the sense way. As soon as we let go and recognize that the way of Spirit is the way of pleasantness, we have been forgiven our sins. The mental attitude has invited the word of God, and it flows forth into our consciousness and erases the erroneous concepts.

Anyone can speak true words and thus be the agent of God in forgiving sin. The little child may do it; the ignorant disciple may do it. The power does not inhere in the individual; the cleansing is through the word. "Already ye are clean because of the word which I have spoken unto you."

This living Word of God is a spiritual principle. It is omnipresent, like the air we breathe.

One small grain of it is more powerful than many tons of dynamite. It is the "assurance of *things* hoped for" that will remove mountains. It is very nigh unto you, even "in thy mouth," as a wise one said. Its premise is that God is good and that His offspring is like unto Him. You have only to recognize this premise in all that you think and do and then speak it forth to get the results promised. There is no respect of persons in God; you are as near the Father as Jesus was if you recognize the principle and speak the true word always.

Six-Day Prayer Treatments

→⇒✕⇐←

I no longer accuse myself and others of sin and evil. Forgiving, I am forgiven and healed.

I daily praise the invisible good that is bringing the ships of prosperity to my harbor.

HOW PRAYER HEALING IS DONE

→⫸✳⫷←

F ROM A STUDY of the foregoing lessons, you
should be convinced that man and the universe are under the creative direction of a supreme being, name it what you will, and that man
needs but to conform to the laws of creative Mind in
order to be healthy, happy, and wise. It logically
occurs to you that all healing methods, whether applied to self or to others, consists in establishing the
unity of the individual and the universal consciousness. No man heals himself or another; the supreme
Mind does the work. "The Father abiding in me
does his works," said Jesus. This is the testimony
of all the truly wise.

The first move in all healing is a rocognition on
the part of the healer and on the part of the patient
that God is present as an all-powerful mind, equal
to the healing of every disease, no matter how bad
it may appear. "With God all things are possible."
The best way to establish unity with the Father-
Mind is by prayer. "God is Spirit," and He has a
kingdom or ruling center in every soul. Do not look
up or out for God, but "pray to thy Father who is
in secret [silently within your own soul], and thy
Father who seeth in secret shall recompense thee."

Many healers use the Lord's Prayer at the beginning
of every treatment. Talk to the Father as if He were
an entity present within you. He is visible to your
soul, and when you have attained the particular
inner confidence called faith, you will realize His
presence as clearly as you realize visible things.
When you have stilled the outer senses and have
become quiet, you are in the mental realm where
thoughts are obedient to the word. Error thoughts
must be told to go, and true thoughts must be called
to take their proper place.

Mental causes are so complex that it is impossible
to point out in all cases the specific thought that
causes a certain disease; but twelve fundamental
mind activities lie at the base of all existence, and
when any one of these is contacted, all the others
respond.

Nearly all sick people lack vital force, hence the
life treatment is good for all. Hate, anger, jealousy,
malice, and the like are almost universal in human
consciousness, and a treatment for love will prove
a healing balm for all.

Fear of poverty burdens most people, and the
prosperity treatment will be effective. Do not be
afraid to use the statements in healing as a whole
or in part; they will always help and never hurt
anyone. Remember that the object of all treatment
is to raise the mind to the Christ consciousness,
through which all true healing is accomplished.

SAMPLE PRAYER TREATMENTS

Fear, anxiety, worry, dread, and suspense—these thoughts cause the mind to become tense, thus shutting out the great helper, the Spirit of truth. Say silently:

I am now free from fear, anxiety, worry, dread, and suspense. I have faith in Thy Holy Spirit, and I trust Thee to protect me, to provide for me, and to bring all my affairs into divine order.

NERVOUSNESS

The mind sends its messages along the nerves; the nerves, forming a network of communication with the brain, get into a chronic crosscurrented condition from the presence of repeated anxious, worried, fearful thoughts, and the many forms of nervousness result. This idea of nervousness must be specifically denied and the truth affirmed. Say silently:

I am not subject to any kind of nervousness. My nerves are harmonized, peaceful, and poised in Spirit and in Truth.

Note: Deny the mental cause first; then the physical appearance. Nervousness is produced by worry, anxiety, and the like. These mental conditions should be healed first; then the secondary state which they have produced in the body must be denied and dissolved, and the perfect condition affirmed.

COLDS, GRIPPE, AND THE INFLUENZAS

Affirm:

*Spirit is not subject to heat or cold. I am Spirit.
I am the positive force of Being, and I put out
of my consciousness all negative thoughts. I do
not believe in the thing called a cold, nor do
I admit for a moment that it has any power over
me. I am Spirit, free-flowing life, and my circulation is equalized in God.*

STOMACH TROUBLES

Prayer:

*My understanding is established in Spirit. I
know the relation between mind and body, between thought and substance. I agree with what
I eat, and what I eat agrees with me. I am at
peace with all men and all things. I do not re-
sist or antagonize anybody or anything. My
stomach is strong, wise, and energetic, and I
always think and speak of it as in every way
capable of doing the work given it to do. I do
not impose upon my stomach by overloading it.
I am guided by divine wisdom in eating and
drinking, and I follow its dictates instead of the
sense appetites. I am no longer anxious about
what I shall eat or what I shall drink. I am not
hurried or worried, but after each meal I rest
from all the cares of life, and I give my stomach
opportunity to do its perfect work under the
divine law.*

ALL LIVER TROUBLES

Prayer:

I am not misjudged, nor do I misjudge others. I do not criticize or condemn. I do not hold bitter, revengeful thoughts against others. I do not think that I have been unjustly treated. God-Mind is my supreme arbiter, and I rest all judgment in the divine law of justice. The swift energy of Spirit now penetrates and permeates every atom of my liver, and it is free to do its perfect work.

KIDNEY, BLADDER, AND URINARY DISORDERS

Prayer:

God is the strength of my life. I do not believe in exhaustion of strength. Strength is always present in supreme completeness, and I am eternally strong. Spirit is the strength of my loins, and my back is free from all thought of burdens. My life is divinely ordered, and I am not afraid of weakness, old age, or death. All the issues of my life are from God, and He is a well of living water within me.

Lustful passions no longer separate me from the pure, spiritual life. My life is lifted up by the Christ Mind, and I am resurrected from the dead. My life is hid with Christ in God.

ALL THROAT AFFECTIONS

Prayer:

All power is given to me, in heaven (mind) and in earth (body). Dominion, control, and mastery are mine by divine right, and I refuse to believe in failure or discouragement.

I am free, and the inspiration of Spirit is poured into my soul. I am quickened by Spirit, and the flesh is obedient. I rejoice and am glad because the joy of Christ is mine. I am filled with Spirit energy, and every cell in my organism is alight with God. I am the resurrection and the life.

SIX-DAY PRAYER TREATMENTS

It is found that the mind establishes a permanent consciousness through six steps or stages, called in Genesis "days."

First, the mind perceives and affirms Truth to be a universal principle. Secondly, faith in the working power of Truth is born in consciousness. Thirdly, Truth takes definite form in mind. Fourthly, the will carries Truth into acts. Fifthly, discrimination is quickened and the difference between Truth and error is discerned. Sixthly, every thought and word is expressed in harmony with Truth.

The seventh "day" represents a peaceful confidence and rest in the fulfillment of the divine law.

By the use of these denials and affirmations for one week a new and more orderly basis of thought is established in mind, and the whole man is harmonized and vitalized. This process often heals obstinate cases, and the six-ray course is recommended in conjunction with the special prayers.

Make your denials as if you were gently sweeping away cobwebs, and make your affirmations in a strong, bold, vehement positive attitude of mind.

Each day's treatment, and the whole course of treatments if necessary, is to be repeated over and over until it manifests its living presence and potency in consciousness.

If you desire to help a patient who will not try or who cannot himself successfully bring his mind into harmonious relations with Principle, think of this person when you hold the daily thought, and Spirit will cause your word to be manifested both in you and in him.

INVOCATION

To precede each day's treatment

I acknowledge Thy presence and power, O blessed Spirit; in Thy divine wisdom now erase my mortal limitations, and from Thy pure substance of love bring into manifestation my world, according to Thy perfect law.

MONDAY

Deny:

I am no longer foolish or ignorant, and the fool-

ishness and the ignorance of ancestry can no
longer be visited upon me.
I am free from the foolishness and the ignorance
of the race and of those with whom I associate.
The foolishness and the ignorance that may
have been treasured up by my own understanding are now erased.

Affirm:

I am wise with the wisdom of infinite Mind
and I have knowledge of all things. I know that
I am pure intelligence and I hereby claim my
divine right to light, life, and liberty in all
goodness, wisdom, love, and purity. Let the
light of wisdom appear and the ignorance of
human thought vanish.

TUESDAY

Deny:

I deny the belief that I have inherited disease,
sickness, ignorance, or any mental limitations
whatsoever. I deny all belief in evil; for God
made all that really is and pronounced it good.
Therefore no such deception as belief in evil
can darken my clear understanding of Truth.
Those with whom I associate can no longer deceive me with their words of consideration and
sympathy. I can no longer deceive myself with
such weakness.

Perish from my world these silly beliefs of

*darkened ignorance. I am now free from them
all, and by my powerful word I hereby destroy
them wholly.*

Affirm:

*God's life is my life, and I vibrate with harmony
and wholeness. I am free with the knowledge
that all is good; I am therefore perfectly whole
and well.*

WEDNESDAY

Deny:

*I deny the belief that I am a child of the flesh
and must suffer for the sins of my forefathers
"unto the third and fourth generation." Perish
all such ignorant beliefs.*

*I deny that I inherited from my ancestors lustful
passions and sensual appetites.*

*I deny the belief that the race can constrain me
to yield to lustful passions and sensual appetites.
I deny the belief that those with whom I associate can constrain me to yield to lustful passions or sensual appetites. I deny my own ignorant belief in such erroneous ideas.*

Affirm:

*God is Spirit and I, the divine image, am Spirit.
I am born of God. God is too pure to behold
iniquity, and I am therefore pure being, without
a tinge of lust or passion.*

THURSDAY

Deny:

I deny that the sins and omissions of my ancestors can influence me in any way. Selfishness, envy, malice, jealousy, pride, avarice, arrogance, cruelty, hypocrisy, obstinacy, and revenge are no part of my present understanding, and I deny all such beliefs in the race, in those with whom I associate, and in my own mind.

Affirm:

I am at peace with all mankind. I truly and unselfishly love all men and women. I now acknowledge the perfect law of justice and equality. I know that "God is no respecter of persons," and that every man and woman is my equal in the sight of the Father.
I do love my neighbor as myself and I will do to others as I would have them do to me.

FRIDAY

Deny:

I deny that I have inherited the consequences of fear from my ancestors, or that the race can constrain me to accept its fears. The fears of those with whom I associate can no longer hold me in sickness or in want, and my own understanding is now fully rid of these illusions.

There is not and cannot hereafter be any fear in or about my bold world.

Affirm:

I am brave and bold with the knowledge that I am Spirit and therefore not subject to any opposing power.

Plenty and prosperity are mine by inheritance from God, and by my steady, persistent word I now bring them into manifestation.

SATURDAY

Deny:

I deny that I inherit any belief that in any way limits me in health, virtue, intelligence, or power to do good.

Those with whom I associate can no longer make me believe that I am a poor worm of the dust. The race belief that nature dominates man no longer holds me in bondage, and I am now free from every belief that might in any way interfere with my perfect expression of health, wealth, peace, prosperity, and perfection in every department of life.

I now, in the sight of Almighty God, unformulate and destroy by my all-powerful word every foolish and ignorant assumption that might impede my march to perfection. My word is the measure of my power. I have spoken, and it shall be so.

Affirm:

I am unlimited in my power and I have increasing health, strength, life, love, wisdom, boldness, freedom, charity, and meekness now and forever.

I am now in harmony with the Father and stronger than any mortal law. I know my birthright in pure Being and I boldly assert my perfect freedom. In this knowledge I am enduring, pure, peaceful, and happy.

I am dignified and definite yet meek and lowly in all that I think and do.

I am one with and I now fully manifest vigorous life, wisdom, and spiritual understanding.

I am one with and I now fully manifest love, charity, justice, kindness, and generosity.

I am one with and I now fully manifest infinite goodness and mercy.

Peace flows like a river through my mind, and I thank Thee, O God, that I am one with Thee!

SUNDAY

"Be still, and know that I am God."

QUESTIONS

QUESTIONS
FOR
TEACH US TO PRAY

By Charles and Cora Fillmore

→»×«←

The God to Whom We Pray

1. How is the spiritual character built?
2. Explain "I go to prepare a place for you."
3. How are we born anew through Christ?
4. How does man awaken the divine nature within him and bring about his union with God?

True Prayer

1. What is true prayer?
2. How does one enter the silence?
3. How are prayers fulfilled?
4. Why does God need man as an avenue of expression.

Intellectual Silence and Spiritual Silence

1. Why do we ask in the name of Jesus Christ?
2. Does salvation come by accepting Jesus as one's Saviour? Explain.
3. Did Jesus make individual effort unnecessary?

4. What is intellectual silence?
5. What is spiritual silence?

Healing through the Prayer of Faith

1. How is faith healing done?
2. How does man develop a deeper faith?
3. What is attention?
4. What is concentration?

Prosperity through Prayer

1. Give your own interpretation of the story of Elisha and the oil.
2. Give the metaphysical interpretation of Elisha, the widow, and the oil.
3. Why is praise so beneficial?
4. Why is daily prayer essential?

Contacting Spiritual Substance

1. What is Spirit substance?
2. How does man appropriate and manifest the invisible substance?
3. How do we gain control of Spirit substance?
4. Why are prosperity demonstrations delayed?

Joyous Prayer

1. How can a metaphysician contact the undiscovered quantities in space?
2. How is the Christ consciousness attained? What is the result?

3. Explain the effect of joy on the mind, body, and affairs.

4. Why must we pray with a purpose?

How to Handle the Psychic Forces of Consciousness

1. What is the only way to handle the psychic forces?

2. What are the three elements of the soul, and what is comprised in each?

3. What effect does the psychic realm have on the emotional nature?

4. What happens to souls who pass on?

5. Explain how Spirit gives messages in dreams and visions.

6. How is man being restored to the heavenly kingdom?

Spiritual Unfoldment Makes Man Master

1. Is man the equal of God?

2. How does man develop his innate abilities?

3. How did Jesus become a master?

4. Why is the unfoldment of love so important in gaining spiritual mastery?

Fulfillment

1. What is the "light of the world"?

2. How did the crucifixion of Jesus save us from sin, sickness, and death?

3. What is the grand fulfillment?

4. Explain the difference between "life" and "blood."

Unfoldment

1. What was the evolution of Jesus?

2. What is your understanding of the Logos?

3. How is the body transformed?

4. How do we partake of the Holy Communion?

Thought Images

1. What are thought images?

2. How do we project thought?

3. Can man have a perfect character? How?

4. Are there short cuts into the kingdom of the heaven?

The Spoken Word

1. Explain the process of creative thought.

2. How does the soul overcome death?

3. What is your understanding of the "ether"?

4. How do we receive a life transfusion?

Thou Shalt Decree

1. What is the effect of man's words?

2. Does an inferiority complex prevent one from expressing sonship?

3. Why do the organs of the body respond to our decrees?

4. Amplify Dr. Alexis Carrel's statement "The only thing that keeps men from living forever is the possession of a brain and nervous system."

Be Strong in the Lord

1. How do we become strong in the Lord?
2. What was Jesus' instruction regarding prayer?
3. Name some helps to entering the silence.
4. Explain the effect of words of praise and failure.

Face to Face with God

1. Why should we speak direct to God?
2. How can we become established in the consciousness of oneness with God?
3. Explain the parable of the prodigal son.
4. Why must we study the life of Jesus?

Not Magic but Law

1. Where is the "kingdom of God"?
2. Was Jesus the only Son of God? Explain.
3. How do we attain the consciousness of eternal life?
4. Why should we look to God as our resource?

Spiritual Soul Therapy

1. What is Spirit psychoanalysis?
2. What determines the character of our soul?
3. Explain the effect of praise on the individual.
4. Does the mental attitude govern spiritual demonstration?

Health and Prosperity

1. How can Spirit manifest itself?
2. How is the immortal body formed?

3. Where is the substance of God?

4. Can we manipulate substance as Jesus did? Explain fully.

Thoughts Are Things

1. What are thoughts?

2. Compare the "ether" of science with the Garden of Eden and the "kingdom of the heavens" of Jesus.

3. Do you agree with Professor Jeans' statement that we live in a universe of waves?

4. How does man form his world?

5. Is there a panacea for the present world conditions?

The Supermind

1. Do all kinds of healers use the same force? Why?

2. What is heaven?

3. What is hell?

4. How did Jesus save us from destructive, discordant conditions?

5. Why do we pray in the name of Jesus Christ?

Cheerfulness Heals

1. How does cheerfulness aid healing?

2. Why does a cheerful attitude bring prosperity?

3. Why is proper diet conducive to health?

4. Why do we bless our money and affairs?

Love Harmonizes

1. How does love adjust man's discords?

2. Explain the law of gravitation.
3. How are great souls developed?
4. Why did Jesus use scientific methods?

Casting Out Fear

1. What is the effect of fear on the body?
2. How do we cast out fear?
3. How do we fulfill the law of our being?
4. What does perfect love mean to you?

Spiritual Hearing

1. How do we hear?
2. Can everyone hear with the "inner ear"? Explain.
3. Is excessive meditation advisable? Why not?
4. Explain the importance of spiritual receptivity.

Light of Life

1. What is the "true light"?
2. Why have the discoveries of modern science about light failed to aid man in his spiritual development?
3. Are light and intelligence one? Explain.
4. What should be the attitude of Truth students in regard to physical science?

Thought Substance

1. How are our prayers answered?
2. Does asking alone bring abundance into manifestation?

3. What is the Spirit of truth?

4. In what way are the laws of hygiene and diet beneficial?

Intensified Zeal

1. Explain the office of the faculty of zeal.
2. What is the cause of "old age"?
3. How did Jesus overcome greed?
4. How do we lay up treasures in the heavens?

The Unreality of Error

1. Why is error unreal?
2. What is the object of man's existence?
3. How is the truth revealed to us?
4. What is matter?

Joy Radiates Health

1. Explain the effect of laughter and joy on health.
2. Where did Solomon turn for judgment?
3. How is happiness attained?
4. How do we find lasting peace?

"Selah!"

1. What does "selah" mean?
2. Why is "God first" the only way to the consciousness of Truth?
3. How does man demonstrate prosperity?
4. What is the meaning of the word "Jehovah"?

Spiritualizing the Intellect

1. How many minds are there? Explain.
2. How do we unify all our forces?
3. Explain the difference between the blessings bestowed by Isaac on Jacob and Esau.
4. What is the intellectual man?
5. What is the proper relationship between the mind and the heart? The mind and the body?
6. Explain the principle of tithing.

The Sevenfold Cleansing

1. Why is humility necessary in spiritual healing?
2. Why must personal egotism be overcome?
3. Name two important steps in spiritual healing.
4. What part did Elisha have in the healing of Naaman?

Prayer and Faith

1. Define prayer in your own words.
2. What does faith mean to you?
3. Why did Paul admonish us to pray without ceasing?
4. What is meant by true spiritual baptism?

The Healing Word

1. Does the "word" have power to heal? Why?
2. What is the "only Son of God"?
3. What does *logos* mean?
4. Can man forgive sin? How?

Index

About the Authors

Charles Fillmore was an innovative thinker, a pioneer in metaphysical thought at a time when most religious thought in America was entirely orthodox. He was a lifelong advocate of the open, inquiring mind, and he took pride in keeping abreast of the latest scientific and educational discoveries and theories. Many years ago he wrote, "What you think today may not be the measure for your thought tomorrow"; and it seems likely that were he to compile this book today, he might use different metaphors, different scientific references, and so on.

Truth is changeless. Those who knew Charles Fillmore best believe that he would like to be able to rephrase some of his observations for today's readers, thus giving them the added effectiveness of contemporary thought. But the ideas themselves—the core of Charles Fillmore's writings—are as timeless now (and will be tomorrow) as when they were first published.

Charles Fillmore was born on an Indian reservation just outside the town of St. Cloud, Minnesota, on August 22, 1854. He made his transition on July 5, 1948, at Unity Village, Missouri, at the age of 93. To get a sense of history, when Charles was eleven, Abraham Lincoln was assassinated; when Charles died, Harry Truman was President.

With his first wife Myrtle, Charles Fillmore founded the Unity movement and Silent Unity, the international prayer ministry that publishes *Daily Word*. Charles and Myrtle built the worldwide organization that continues their work today, Unity School of Christianity. Through Unity School's ministries of prayer, education, and publishing, millions of people around the world are finding the teachings of Truth discovered and practiced by Charles and Myrtle Fillmore.

Charles Fillmore was a spiritual pioneer whose impact has yet to be assessed. No lesser leaders than Dr. Norman Vincent Peale and Dr. Emmet Fox were profoundly influenced by him. Dr. Peale borrowed his catchphrase *positive thinking* from Charles Fillmore. Emmet Fox was so affected by Fillmore's ideas that he changed his profession. From an engineer, he became the well-known writer and speaker.

Charles Fillmore—author, teacher, metaphysician, practical mystic, husband, father, spiritual leader, visionary—has left a legacy that continues to impact the lives of millions of people. By his fruits, he is continuously known.

→)×(←

Cora Fillmore was born Cora Dedrick on December 15, 1876, and came to work as secretary to Charles around 1905. Ordained a minister in 1918, she served as director of Silent Unity for a brief period and then became private secretary to both Charles and Myrtle until Myrtle's death in October 1931. In December 1933, she became Charles' second wife when they were married at the home of Lowell Fillmore at Unity Farm. The following day they left on an extensive tour of the country to lecture on the teachings of Unity!

In 1939 Cora served on the faculty of Unity School of Christianity. In addition to cowriting this book, she compiled two others from the writings of Charles, *Keep a True Lent* and *Atom-Smashing Power of Mind*, and wrote *Christ Enthroned in Man*. She made her transition on January 29, 1955.

Printed in the U.S.A.

47-0656-2M-3-02